The Ruins of Paris

TOPOGRAPHICS

The Ruins of Paris

Jacques Réda

Translated by MARK TREHARNE

REAKTION BOOKS

Published by Reaktion Books Ltd
11 Rathbone Place, London W1P 1DE, UK

First published in English 1996

First published in French as *Les Ruines de Paris*
© Editions Gallimard, 1977

English language translation © Reaktion Books, 1996
This work has been published with the support of the
French Ministry of Culture

Translated by Mark Treharne

Designed by Ron Costley
Photoset by Parker Typesetting Service, Leicester
Printed and bound in Great Britain by
Biddles Ltd, Guildford and King's Lynn

British Library Cataloguing in Publication Data

Réda, Jacques
The ruins of Paris. – (Topographics)
1. Travel 2. Europe – Description and travel
I. Title
914

ISBN 0 948462 93 0

The Ruins of Paris

I

The stealthy footsteps of the heretic

In winter, around six o'clock, I need no coaxing to walk down the left side of the avenue through the public gardens, and I stumble into benches and small bushes because my gaze is utterly absorbed by a sky as incomprehensible as the approach of love. Its almost faded colour is not definable: a really dark turquoise perhaps, the deep condensation of a light that eludes the eye and becomes the icy fire of the soul it invades. Noiseless convoys of clouds scurry, noiselessly, across lakes. Lightning would be less of a shock than this explosion of unending silence. Stormy glints do in fact jostle these pastry pavilions and, further off, the whole spectacle gathers in density like a powder keg about to explode. Everywhere the subtlety and the flickering furnace of love; and everywhere there are branches to celebrate this smouldering fire of nightfall: subdivisions of the darkness tearing itself out from the mass of singing trees, seeking to lose itself among them but stumbling against the narrowest branch tips and cracking on the high notes. The same voice is in my head, and the same monotonous density. At times we can become possessed by some compelling obsession with transmutation – by dint of studying some spectacle, walking in its vicinity, entering blind substance that shines with knowledge. As if a man, stopping momentarily in his tracks and setting his gaze on the sky, did not himself extend beyond the irresistible envelopment of stars. This is the moment I stumble against the hoops bordering the grass. Somehow or other I eventually reach the Place de la Concorde. Space suddenly becomes maritime. Even with almost no wind there is a whiff of weighing anchors in the air. And, against the columns, below the balustrades guarded by lions, the swaying sailing vessels of a Claude painting surge up, the timber of their hulls and masts, the rigging, the canvas whistling and creaking, tearing the smoky flag that is for ever unfurling above the city. So I walk along as if

I were on a beach, through this fallow land. And perhaps it is the uncertain evening light that opens up such a perspective to my eyes, though it remains merged with the stone and the din of Paris. For in broad daylight, especially during the badly tamed months (February, March, November), when the air pales as it does on the fringes of heathland and marshes, the streets cut through the glow of a sandy estuary; with every step you take a pearly shimmer is on the point of rising up between the dunes, the heart jumps, and whole forests in transhumance park themselves at crossroads then slip out of sight in a single leap, like the unicorn. An elemental yet soothing natural wildness has survived on these monuments. Taking refuge in the sky, the most sensitive part of this world still, it affects even marble, which is impervious to time and season. So an angle juts out like a mast amid this sea of metamorphoses, hoisting up palaces, in the splendour of the first day of creation. Teams of green bronze horses fly off; the centuries, lost between two antediluvian tides of ferns, seem at the mercy of their own fragility, and human hope, wide-eyed, seems to confront its solitude. Now night has really fallen. The English bookshop beneath the arcade has just put out its lights. As if it were muffled in velvet, the tragic injunction *My Lord!* is heard, and then no further sound between the pages closed again on crimes, mountains and the vocalic palpitations of nightingales. Deserted and burnt to a cinder now, the public gardens brood below a terraced walk. The walk itself is no less deserted beneath the old leaded gold reflected from the fronts of its buildings, and it follows a straight course like a strange burst of fanfare from the Age of Reason, creating fanatical laws in the inflexible space between parallel lines and the spiteful abstraction of infinity. Down a few steps and happily you are on solid ground again: plain, humble, hard ground on which children, by dragging those heavy park seats that vibrate and jump around, have traced loops of narrow-gauged railway track. The undergrowth in some woods seems similarly devoid of greenery because the beech trees sap all the available nourishment in the soil. But here it seems that the trees have been set without roots, standing only by virtue of their size and weight, like pieces of furniture. The stone ballast, the packed soil and the continual rub of foot-leather on the paws of mastodons are not an adequate explanation. Fairly large tracts of this ground have remained untouched for months except by the stealthy footsteps of the heretic, and yet grass, for ever ready to make a spontaneous appearance, even on church towers, is obstinate in its refusal to grow here. One spring morning you think you have seen moss growing: then before midday it has vanished into thin air. So you are left to imagine that this poverty and cleanliness are intentional, but it is not the cleanliness of hygiene: it belongs to the convent. All the same, this excessive austerity grants itself some compensation as far as the height of things is concerned, when the dozing greyness between the branches dreams of every possible colour and this humble, inky wood feeds a spiritual flame, untouched above the apocalyptic steam of the great cauldron. Not a soul. The surrounding rumble of traffic spreads out, bulges up into a dome of hubbub and fades away. Beneath the noise I can hear the stray music of a little resident school of flutes accompanying the frozen prancing of the horses on the merry-go-round. Nowhere, apart from the few frescoes from which they seem to originate, do you have a better depiction of the grace of frolicking animals: the inevitably exaggerated awkwardness with which this grace is captured makes it truer to life, painted in the real colours of real horses against fences where a whole floating sky is leaning, there to be touched: bright orange, deep black, smoky white, and those rather fiercely dilated nostrils transforming the air into smells, images, memories and desires from which we are barred. They prance naïvely, gently, in the shadows, prolonging the still lingering enchantment of the children no longer there, while my footsteps echo in counterpoint to the fluted music. The music fades away, nostalgia or broken gaiety like the soft flutings at the close of Fauré's *Requiem*, and in a limping movement of crystal glasses and silverware, this immense old people's tea-party plunges towards the absolute in spirals, like a merry-go-round. Simultaneously, in the dust haze of a forge, I become aware of thousands of ghosts carried off at different speeds along a single line. Each one of them in turn becomes double, and immediately each double flies backwards, doubles back on itself, and sends out yet another immediately doubling double so that in the end this disorder balances out into a pattern and slides smoothly towards the station over the accommodating slack play of the footbridge that grates between the whirling sky and its reflections as they sluggishly unwind themselves in the water. These ghosts ought to scare me as I pass through them were I – with no fixed timetable in mind and straying from my path – not in fact even more unreal, and possibly more terrifying than they are. At the centre of the pool, the imprisoned nymph of the fountain shakes her wild hair in every direction. I step into the pallid mud of a building site as it vibrates like a dredge beneath the lamps. To frustrate the curious gaze it has been boarded up, but (as with all barriers) there are holes in the boards. Yet as I pass by I merely take in what little there is to be seen – the usual diabolical excavation, and it no longer interests me. What does interest me now is to follow the will of the moon and to linger behind in my tracks for as long as possible, like a beast in the middle of the bridge. For to the north a gap has appeared in the dregs, widening the icy gulf where two stars tap out the brief signals of their optical telegraphy. I stand looking at the two shores as they recede in shreds and steam horizontally in front of the moon. There are two ring-shape bruises – blue and black-brown – surrounding them completely: they pour phosphorescence onto the clouds. A dog with things on his mind passes by, avoiding me as if I were a wolf. And I could indeed start howling to my heart's content since I am there on my own apart from the dog and the noise of motors that a sudden shaft of moonlight annihilates with its top C. The moon has been polished with zealous frenzy. You would grab hold of the edges were it not for fear of leaving finger-marks or of being reduced in a second to a pinch of ashes, for she burns, not like the sun's heat, calculable in vast numbers of degrees, but by the purely lyrical effect of her light, which inflames the brains of madmen and burns them to cinders. That's right – I am thinking of a Lady. With increasing vagueness and despair no doubt, but thinking of her constantly. I start walking again. Despair does not exist for a walking man, provided he really walks without turning round all the time to chatter away to someone else, pitying himself, showing off. Other people listen to you for a long time in fact, and seem to agree with what you say. Then, with the harmlessly sorry look of victims, sooner or later they catch you out on something and hang you from the nearest nail. This is why I am walking fast and straight in front of me towards the open country and the thickets around Les Invalides. You come across rabbits as early in the journey as the rue de Babylone. Bells chime behind the thick walls I brush against as I go by: touching them brings relief and disposes me to reflection. But on what should I reflect when the sky turns turbulent from far away in the plains and the clod-hopping wind smacks my face with its load of cold soft earth? I am going home. There are eggs, cheese, wine and a stack of records, and at the push of a button you can bring out the bass line. So I move on, pizzicato. Am I happy? Sad? Am I moving towards an enigma, a sense of meaning? I don't try too hard to find out. I have become the vibration of those bass strings, tautened like hope and as resonant as love.

Noiselessly and almost wordlessly

The two stairways up this deep black iron bridge meet at the top. I take the one on the left and hardly have I reached the top than I bang my head against a lamp-post. At once the whole sky, grey and blue-drenched, fills with tower-blocks. They sparkle. And the bigger they become the more the sky itself expands. I would undoubtedly prefer this civilization of lamp-posts and footbridges to stay in place permanently, but if it only takes me going by for them to topple in a minute, then this world will go on transforming itself eternally. The only people in front of me were two little girls dressed in red. Each determinedly chose which stairway she would take without a glance at the other or with any heed of the threatening surroundings in which their colour sings out: the depot looming over the scene like the wall of a fortress; the railway cutting widening out beneath the bridge and its unyielding cellar-like grating. Metallic and wooden objects among heaps of coal and bundles of papers, some obscure residue from the railway, strew soot onto the tracks down there, but by contrast there is a polyphonic heap of oil drums, many of them – yellow, blue, green. Chance, or whatever, has willed the rightness of the way they are placed. I walk back the same way and listen. Above the Parc Montsouris the sky shimmers ceaselessly, breaking like crystal glass. On the other side of the bridge I cannot even find any streets: nothing but trees from some other century, and mud ploughed up into slopes reaching towards more tower-blocks. A few drops of rain scatter and sail about the place. In the distance, a single blob of red from the little girls who are bending down with their arms around their necks.

It has been raining heavily for a few minutes and everything is fresh. The downpour continues to straddle the rooftops towards the suburbs, with the roomy gesture of a young girl holding up her skirt so that she can run faster. Deep in every gap in the walls, trees are sprucing up themselves again. The seventeenth-century masonry on every transparent shop and *café-tabac* shows up like new, and in other places the temporary plasterwork around boarded windows weighs down heavily on courtyards stuffed to their portals with crates. The streets dither and then get going again, with a preference for conversation and the sale of things to eat and drink: Russian bread rolls, *vin du Carmel*, and bright red salami sausages with the Hebrew stamp-mark from the Grand Rabbinate of Paris. The things you see through the intriguing cracks in the boarding never change: the imperial nettles from the dark recesses of childhood, but also the giant yellow-gold mechanical digger, standing there askew against the sky like a dredger thrown onto the rocks by the sea. In the depths of the air, mobile and drenched but still blue, the boulevards act like river-locks, then start moving out in every direction from République to the Bastille as if they were heading vertically for the future.

As we move forward like two gleaners among these flattened ruins in the rue de Belleville we are not really looking for anything in particular, but we pick up anything we see and end up with two window frames that are probably unusable, but in almost perfect condition. A little further ahead is a competitor with his eye on hexagonal floor bricks; the price has risen today to nearly eighty francs per square metre. 'I've already emptied more than two skips of them', he tells us. He has also taken an oak main-beam, and there is still another like it among the rubble. But the Portuguese clearance team have damaged it by heating their billycans near it. And either out of curiosity or justifiable necessity they have also broken open the door of the old aqueduct inspection point. This old *Regard* formerly stood neglected between two rows of garages, and it now remains untouched by the mechanical diggers because it is fenced in. But fences can be crossed, and the presence of this smashed doorlock even entitles us to go down inside. A staircase leads to a small shallow pool in which a tiny amount of water echoes like jingling keys beneath the vault and a sewer tunnel disappears off into the heavy darkness. The glimmer of light up in the lantern dome is gradually fading with the oncoming night. So we go up again to cart off our window frames and a few handfuls of postcards. Several of these are addressed to Jeanne or Louise Forgeron and they date from the turn of the century. Since they bear female signatures and portraits of *La Belle Georgette* enveloped in transparent veils we tend to regard them as both ambiguous and outmoded. But perhaps our reaction is too worldly wise. Others picture the usual cathedrals. In other places we discover impeccably kept geography exercise-books, the remains of toys (a dog, a piece of rail from a train-set), pier-glasses and really old pieces of marquetry work. It would be good to be able to save it all but it would only get stuck there indefinitely down in our cellar and distress us even more. Besides, in five minutes' time there will be nothing left to see of this wreckage. The weary pink sky is still holding out above the zinc rooftops, but around the tiny squares the cafés have already put out their lights and the streets are being swallowed up amid the whirling acacia trees.

Everything shrivels up at the top of the rise and crumbles like plaster. Narrow streets tumble down on both sides. After a while they stretch on monotonously. It's better to stay in the middle, closer to the sky, which is even more impressive than usual because it is silently exploding like a mountain, splashing the rooftops and the cobbles with the blue of its living gaze, observing the scene. People, with their slightly swollen Sunday heads, are moving about like clouds. Some of the oldest among them who no longer care about time eye me shrewdly: I am clearly a stranger here; no-one else would think of taking a photograph of the barber's shop for its particular shade of pink. But this curiosity fades almost at once because of a general need for indifference and an unhurried pace of life. Small shops still flourish here. Groups of people queue up in front of the baker's or beneath the golden flaring nostrils of the horse-butcher's sign. The things that capture my interest in the general store are not the books on display but cheap plastic toys: mountain infantry-men in snow uniforms, with hunting horns; apple-green barrows filled with dusty sweets. Once more I find myself conscious of the presence, up against the Butte-aux-Cailles, of a real mountain range, with this bounding sky and its passes tiered up in terraces, and its way of coming close up to you like an infinitely affectionate being. This is why people here move around unhurriedly, noiselessly and almost wordlessly, in a numb feeling of hope before the devastating event of midday.

I am not quite sure what they will think about it afterwards, but for the moment they show no surprise. I have got hold of the tune because the words are firmly in my mind. They are very obliging and sing them over again for me. I note them down on a scrap of envelope, thank them and go off. The unfortunate American contamination in this children's counting song is obvious:

Maillemailloupette,
Bo, be, fiou,
Superman, waterman,
Fi, fai, stop.

It is unfortunate, but at the same time intriguing. You wonder through what channels these concertina forms of language are handed down and spread in the underground world of children, and if this world is really where speech first becomes inadvertently contaminated, far more than by what the laws laid down by theory have to say, by things plugged on the radio or by the books that no one reads anyway. At the same time, some traditions remain untouched. I remember another song that I heard in the Palais-Royal, sung as the accompaniment to a rather complicated ritual to do with the handling of a skipping-rope. That time I didn't risk asking about it in case I frightened them – they were tiny girls. The refrain went like this:

En avant, la femme du sergent,
En arrière, la femme du pompier,
Tout autour, la femme du tambour . . .

but before it there was an incessantly repeated motif (quaver, dotted crochet, semiquaver, rest, then the quaver again and so on . . .) both monotonous and compelling, like the rhythmic hum of a spinning-wheel or sewing-machine. And this motif from the depths of time would be transmitted. Other little girls of seven with their austere bacchic frenzy and the authority of priestesses would preserve the celebration of ancient Pan on the deadened streets of Paris.

Glowing raspberry pink, but pink like a water-ice – a sorbet fallen from its cornet and rolling about in the dust – the sun is in the throes of dilating in a way that would be frightening were it not for this element of holiday colour in the background, soon to change to the colour of old silk, crumbling away rather than suddenly falling apart. The total indifference of passers-by is incomprehensible. It seems to me that we should gather in a circle on the terrace, dancing and shouting, or else observe a hieratic silence and not stir a hair. What would happen if I were to climb onto the balustrade with my arms spread in a gesture of consecration or farewell? Perhaps I'd be taken for a mystical exhibitionist or a mad surveyor of the skies, but no one would really be bothered by it. All the same, I avoid such antics, even in private. There was just that evening when I officiated like a priest at the top of an Aztec mound in the Yvelines, at the far end of an empty golf-course. It wasn't long before I started to feel disapproval for my histrionics. So what is it that I need? It is this: that brief moment of elation as I come out of the Tuileries, when for a second I am unaware of the fact that I am someone looking at something that can no longer be called the sun, as it snatches up the mysterious obelisk and I stand rooted to the spot in the pink immensity, for reasons that have nothing to do with ecstasy or with terror.

On the water, hammered out like iron and on which you could walk, there is no one. And then, on the cobbled embankment that stretches on for more than three hundred feet, half-way between the canal and the wall where patches of moss draw attention to various inaccessible footholds, I light on the only recent object to have been left there on the ground – a single crutch. My footsteps falter but I shall not recoil. I am already quite a distance from the steps that lead down to the canal from the Bastille, its column standing there like a distress signal in the slopeless, uncentred flabby air. I would rather stay down here by the canal, the hard-surfaced water and this criminal esplanade. It is less frightening. Over on the other bank, near a machine plant breathing away like an enormous grazing cow, there are men in yellow and blue rushing about. They would be of no use at all if something dreadful were to happen but their presence is none the less reassuring (and accompanied by images of the tragic events that have led to it lying there, I skirt around this malignant object and move on towards the spot where the lock blocks the canal and the dark tunnel begins).

It is no use reminding myself that the young Proust must have capered about beneath these trees: the whole district still stinks from the cash of crooked business deals. Fraudulent dealing on a very much humbler scale is in evidence here on Thursdays when the stamp-dealers come, but the real scandal is here every day as people keep coming back to drive themselves to exhaustion in front of telephones and blotting-pads. So once again I get off the bus in this place. At the Rond-Point, alarmed by the drastic crush of people, a lady with some mysterious green stuff in a bag balances precariously on her bicycle. She has come from Montrouge or Clamart where a few vegetable plots still manage to survive behind the concrete, and she must be going to Saint-Lazare to catch a train. With her heavy brown jumper and navy-blue skirt she seems the only decent human being around, amid this whorehouse medley of expensively dressed men and women dragging their dogs along. She is not quite sure which direction to take, but she is certainly not going to ask anyone. In the end she will have no difficulty getting to Maurecourt, where her sister lives. And then in the evening, after retrieving her bicycle at the station, emboldened, she will set off again in the opposite direction, without any further worry about crowds, Palaces and Arches, wobbling a bit on her bike because her bag is now stuffed with rhubarb.

An iron chain dragging in the grass doesn't keep people out. But then the embankment narrows as it runs along a wall and stumbles up against a very low rectangular tunnel, a dead end. Seated on the ground, I get the feeling that this huge deserted stretch of dirty water comes up to my mouth. It glistens. Back there above the Saint-Denis canal, the hill-slopes turn to dust. The only surviving habitation is this outpost of trees. The sun stirs in their leaves, feebly, like a hand cut off from the body, and causing the sky to explode. On the right, below the last bridge where a group of black men are guffawing with laughter, I saw three fishermen on the bank of the side channel. There are two more opposite me, completely lost, motionless in the consuming brightness. I expect them to vanish at any moment, and with them the ancient catastrophe of industrial buildings with their enraged rooftops, the chalk tower-blocks, the footbridges and the barges suspended in the air like dead horses that never stop swelling. It would all be swallowed up at once in the devouring tranquillity of this corner of the world, and I would be able to stay here for ever.

In the rue des Tournelles my attention is captured by La Boucherie du Génie. From further away come gusts of something like the beat of a tango. And as I walk down the middle of the deserted street the stubborn old rhythm and the tune do become distinct. I come to a café in which I can see no one apart from a middle-aged couple dancing by the bar with studied intensity, all but drowned in this Sunday immensity. I walk on with my eyes on the sky because slate-coloured clouds are breaking and there will be rain. The light that announces this, like a blind man forgetful of nothing, fingers the rooftops and the trees, which have suddenly increased in size and drawn nearer.

The gleam of light that has settled over the Luxembourg is red, bright as a forge battling against a stifling wind. But to say red is not enough, I need to add rapid, even though it also seems forever still. But there is good reason for this. There is no better way of conveying it than a notion of giddy suspense enveloped by rapidity and giving birth to the deepening crimson of this gleaming light. The shadow, by contrast, is very slow to deepen and the air becomes increasingly raw. None of this stops the city from disclosing those tropical inclinations, which are already so obvious in broad daylight in the avenue Emile-Zola, the rue Caulaincourt and that purely metaphysical stretch of the rue d'Estrées: an exuberant species of plants related to the acacia, the handsome paulownias and the catalpas that surround the thrones of empresses. The unctuous asphalt starts to curve like an equator with tyres sculling around on it, and the huge muffled drum-rolls of the clouds broadcast the unfathomable presence of the word Gabon. But the most convincing element in this sudden transference of latitudes is the deepened shade of ochre on the fronts of buildings, even the Law Faculty, saturated after the downpour in a rotting decomposition from Brazil. Were it not for the considerable care that is taken, the vegetation would run rampant, but you can't control it all, and as I pass by I stroke the thick tufts of grass that burst out freshly between the stones along the Panthéon behind the statue of Rousseau.

for Sébastien Kerr

He is wearing blue trousers and a leather jacket, probably not real leather but it is new and looks solid. The cap with the City arms is pulled down well over his face. In supreme control of the water sources in his territory, he unleashes torrents from the sky into the hollows of the gutter. He stands there talking to a colleague who is still a trainee in a soft aquatic dialect without letting go of that distinguished tool of his trade – his twig broomstick. I have seen others like him who have inspired me to tragic emotion because of the way that destiny revealed itself in their posture of captive kings. The lesson offered me by this man is no less noble for being of a more republican nature. He reincarnates the potential contained in the idea of a republic: a people, a senate, lictors, a sense of virtue and the way its indivisible dignity is carried over to people whose task it is to work on building, city maintenance and the upkeep of parks. As evidence of a skill, and thus of the necessity of the beauty of a function, this roadsweeper's broom is there to re-abolish hierarchies and privileges from the Etoile to Alma and to re-establish an element of common sense in streets overrun by Executives in putty-coloured suits who sign documents and use telephones. Some of these executives even try to camouflage themselves, pass themselves off as artists or members of the Resistance, but not one of them gets anywhere near the honest appearance of the roadsweeper as a useful and free being, and as a symbol. A symbol of what? Not of Established Order, but rather of an evolving and therefore republican order with its universal extension into a citizenship that holds sway with a host of peculiarities that command respect or hold their own ground, a host of ways of speaking within a single common language, each of them active in its own nook. I ought now to draw some clear political conclusions from all this, but that is not my job. My job is to see, to describe and then to sweep up, without undue zeal but conscientiously, like this Black colleague of mine.

All sorts of rubbish is floating about in the canal underneath the moveable bridge, its machinery thick with grease and with hardly a cog on the wheels. The shape of a bottle can still be easily recognized, but the flabby dead forms brought alive by the plopping water turn the blood cold. And here is where you see it, less than a hundred metres past the rue de Crimée and its ancient barbarity, the living embodiment of the new barbarity. There it is, opposite warehouses with whole bushes projected from their brick-pillared corners, thrusting itself up in a single narrow block over more than thirty floors, white in the blue sky which is raging like a furious angel. Why would it not assume this appearance of a block of flats? So it does. Clouds go scurrying over its head in terror. And knowing nothing of angels or blocks of flats perhaps they divulge its name. Then something else happens on the same path they are following, across the Canal de l'Ourcq: a sort of slow-motion eruption of a mountain of smoke, as blue as a segment of the Juras, and we – a passing postman and myself – stare at each other in amazement at the exuberance of the world.

The sole aim of the world is to glory in itself unceasingly and to glorify us too, even amid our despair and in death, since it pushes along these shining clouds above our heads and our poems. I see them, day and night, over the dome of Les Invalides, unfurling through all the indescribable shades of blue. It is true, we are placed here like an encampment of canvas tents and the wind of eternity rushes on. But anyone who takes a moment's notice can believe that light is a form of greeting, that it has chosen the deep and fragile mirror of our eyes. Such is the modest elevation of my thoughts as I wait for the bus in front of that monumental pact achieved in stonemasonry between Mansart and Bruant; and up in the sky is the breath of the gods. (Everything passes: the wind, the gods, eyes, stone, clouds, buses, and at different speeds, but in order to show that splendour lasts on – and peace be on earth to those other clouds that lie in store for us.)

The air, already a blaring white, turns dazzling when one of those fierce black clouds breaks. Sitting at the edge of the small shelter in the middle of a circular square, I come to the conclusion that this is still perhaps my favourite kind of weather, together with those evenings that come to an end in a sort of crazy tenderness beneath the golden weight as it becomes heavier and heavier and when the shadows disappear more and more quickly and end up meeting, merging, submerging the world and returning it to peace. If the wind were to die down it would immediately start to rain, but very briefly, for the wind merges as many skies into one sky as there are registers and stops on an organ. The bourdon stops growl over my head and over the warehouses; a background note of *vox celesta* grows louder amid the rigid framework of the gasometers. Before me is a walled street, deserted right up to the black hole where the bridge is: I walked down it in the opposite direction last year and, despite the handsome warehouse in well-tarred wood, I know almost no other street in Paris as completely destitute and sinister as this one. Before the fifteenth *arrondissement* was ruined, we witnessed the unexpected and somewhat dazed encounter, amid a silent jumble of shacks, between Cervantes and Plato. But disaster is often like this, merely a disaster for its victims, pitiful, whereas in this street the drabness hides a sense of coldly premeditated crime. In addition to the changed street name, they have done what they could to exorcize the unavoidable soulless fascination of the place, fearsome but mysteriously fraternal. At the other end of the street there is that huge crucifix, and here the first relay point in six hundred metres of desert. Since everything is part and parcel of everything else, it was even necessary for the bistro here to be baptised, thus adding a conceited and rather mockingly blasphemous note to the sinister nature of the place. But I have not yet stopped for a drink at the *Royal Gospel* . . .

Because both her arms are raised over one half of Paris, this woman seems to be making an imploring gesture, but it is a gesture of enthusiasm, and right next to her another dark mass of clouds moves off in applause. The vehement colours of the sky a while back are now turning into bruise marks. So once again I have seen the submerged glimmer of daylight rise up from the Panthéon. Tiny people in tiny numbers – it is Sunday – scurry on the steps like ants. And although, like me, they are dressed in the clothes of today, their agitated flight beneath the columns creates the impression that they have stepped out of time. Meanwhile, the wind up there that was puffing on the blue to stir it up into this red, stoking it with purple twigs, goes on rummaging about beneath the clumps of bushes and the metal scrap of waste ground. As always, lying there in the old embittered grass that fiercely clings to life, the same boot, and for me, as I peer through the cracks in the boards and see nothing but the same old wall behind esplanades of rubble, the same sense of hope. Yet here, in the rue Mesureur, where this tattered poster screams out, there is something new: it pictures a slim blonde lady acrobat, starkers except for her panties, in exactly the same pose as the woman in the clouds who is now scudding away, but with a massive revolver aimed at the small of her back.

As the greyness softly darkens

I have unexpectedly discovered a garden square near the rue Desnouettes. My initial plan was to go to the Sacré-Coeur, to Montmartre is what I really mean. And here I am near the Place Balard and the helicopter base where a stone slab commemorates the feat of Henri Farman – a kilometre's closed circuit flight in a Voisin biplane with an Antoinette motor on 13 January 1908. This is the sort of thing I note down (when I start stalling) about matters that basically don't interest me. Perhaps it is an attempt to exalt myself through some kind of hoarding instinct: my worry about padding along so many streets to no end. Issy-les-Moulineaux seems to me to be more insipid than depressing. I study a brand new hotel, the sort of thing that the builders of the Pyramids would construct today. These ultra-modern constructions really do have something very Egyptian about them in their timeless and funerary way. They are as overwhelming as they are reassuring. But no doubt they will resist the passage of time less well than the tombs of Egypt. The first thing to go will be the outside lift that moves up and down like a bubble from which it must be possible to see the Sacré-Coeur. Anybody is free to try this voluptuous vertigo, but I realize that too late. I drag on, about to stop and read the headlines of the old newspapers which are also dragging about on the ground and are quickly driven into a heap by the really sharp wind. On my way back I bring to mind the shock I would normally feel beneath the Petite-Ceinture railway line that crosses the rue de Vaugirard at the sight of those coaches in the depot and the heaving grass embankment. But everything is silent. It is at this point that I chance on my garden square, quiet and flat, stuck away at the back of blocks of flats. It has a concrete hillock, straight out of some zoo of Nubian monkeys, actually planted there for children by a committee of town-councillors with psycho-pedagogic pretensions. Not only do the children not care two hoots about it and stick to the sandpit, but the hillock itself makes no impression against the sheer drop of the blinded house fronts that surround it, as the sun lingers and warms itself like an old man on the park benches and the deserted dreamy grass. I realize that this is where I should have stayed and waited. Some other time. There is very little time left before the day ends, and nothing urges me on or makes me stop. I go into a cinema. Champollion was the subject of a fine documentary – Egypt again. I leave. It is dark now, and here is the street where she who remains my sister – according to the mystic Numbers – once lived. Very few glimmers of light. All the bakers' along the rue Lecourbe are emptying and it doesn't even occur to me to buy bread, nor would I have the courage for it.

Deep in the greyness of this afternoon light there is a lot of yellow – November – and when I look up (because a lady really has exploded all over the place on a real banana skin right there on the pavement) it is as if I myself were slipping into a photo with no sense of perspective in it, with the rue de Rennes flattened up against the Tour Montparnasse with long volleys of mist. Without even the time to think 'Manhattan 1917, transportation of troops', there I am in a blink of surprise. So in the past when I used to leaf over those heavy shiny albums in search of the same images (the skyscrapers of smoke and the filthy mud of the Argonne at the end of it all), on the other side of the Atlantic and more than fifty years back, I was moving towards this present intrusion into an entirely different destiny. But I don't have to immerse myself in the reasons behind such things: it is enough that they happen to me and disturb me; let's leave it at that. I look away and see the lady once more, fortunately unharmed but still pale with fright. Then a window display catches my eye with its big boxes of pastels: they can inflect the infinite variety of everything with their different shades. I am hypnotized and it wouldn't take long before they drove me half crazy.

As you come up from the Porte d'Orléans and get about half way along the avenue du Maine, there is this huge ledge where the sky swells out and rolls along as lightly as a bubble against the Tour Montparnasse. Less than fifty metres away the city starts to reconstitute itself, but we've known that for a long time now. But knowing doesn't really change anything, however certain the knowledge: step back a few paces and you find yourself on the very outer limits again, the point at which everything bursts forth at the edge of a luminous void. The Tour Montparnasse has altered none of this because it points its top storeys upwards, like the tip of a gauging instrument, and plunges them into the unknown. Looking for a more concrete image, one might say that the first sight of the ocean can be glimpsed beyond this tarmac ledge, yet unobtrusively and somehow without any waves; it is reduced, after an infinite expanse of mud and soft sand, to this delicate streak of fire which flickers and which will capsize like a boat beneath an excess of sail and blue sky. It is like a turbulence of bright light signalling the open sea from far off, in the dilated air, but what in fact appears can very well turn out to be simply a marshalling yard with its fanning jets of gleaming railway track. And in fact where I am now is very near the network of railway lines at Montparnasse. And I long for earth-bound paths that follow the railway line rather than this metaphysical fantasy of the void and plenitude, of ends and fresh beginnings, however much the end of the street, at cloud level, gives on to an imminent vision of them. But soon, on my left, I reach the rue de l'Ouest, and then the rue du Château, the Arabianized bar counters and the Jewish delicatessen, a crowd of pedestrians not much given to conversation, strolling along like *flâneurs* (with a flannel-like air about them into the bargain), and lingering in long queues. They are signing a petition against the proposed motorway: it would thrash down across this sombre, impoverished yet quietly self-contained neighbourhood and its inhabitants like a huge concrete truncheon.

With friendly presences already passing across it in the near distance, the inhabitants of sunlight, lingering, passing and returning, the air remains meticulously carved out of this crumbly, dull substance – the winter daylight of Paris. On the corner of the rue de Vaugirard, the only surviving sign of the former *faubourg* is a small butcher's shop – the crossroads could just as well belong anywhere, as could the building I observe lower down the street with its inevitable balcony of farewell on the fifth floor. It would come as no surprise to see a hand appear there again, but this time to beckon me, and were this to happen, time would once more turn to a long stretch of sloping sand, very pale and fine-grained as forest sand can be, still shining in the night that wants us to separate and which once again is prolonged for ever by a hand raised in this gesture of farewell. And I am now reduced to a mere wayward memory, losing itself in street after street as far as the dazzling light of the bridges, among passers-by dreamt up by the winter sun.

Leaning on my handlebars in a particularly pensive mood, I have the idea of creating a Union for the Preservation of Waste Land. The UPWL. This poem (if that is what it is) will serve as its manifesto, or rather as a preamble for the project since I myself will be taking no part in it, incapable as I am of being in the streets and in the offices of such an organization at one and the same time. So let it remain a kind of guild, a kind of vague waste land itself, without statutes and subscriptions, so that neither the press nor the politicians can lead it astray, despite the useful way in which they can keep property developers in check or even get them thrown in clink when one of their building sites assaults a former piece of waste ground or creates another. This is, none the less, the only positive side to their ravages: in the interval between the demolition brought about by bulldozers and the construction of those blocks of residential flats that seem to come straight out of some old album of homage to Lyautey (to the point where whole hectares of the fifteenth *arrondissement* implement the colonial ideals of concrete blocks in Fès or Rabat), there is occasionally a fairly long lapse of time during which you can see the regrowth of the flourishing vegetation of ruined places through the loosening boards. Of course I would not want all waste ground to be preserved; it would mean looking after the crowds of vagrants and homeless. But I note that occasionally (and infrequently, to be honest) substitute squares and gardens are set up on waste land. Now this is what I am up in arms about, and it arouses protest in the rebellious souls of men and cats alike. At least half these areas should be left to run wild, even with the danger that could come from these mounds of planks and plaster and the health risks of these piles of filth all over the place and the dirty water. So just in case, get your children vaccinated against tetanus and typhoid, and they will be perfectly safe. And we will also take care not to pull

38

down the sheet-metal hoardings and their heavy wooden supports, which can last for up to one hundred years. For whatever pleasure there is in wandering about in an area of waste ground, the initial attraction is to see it spreading out through the chinks in the hoarding as a space for meditation. What it has to teach us lies in the presence of its sullen wilderness alone, and it is better to refrain from deriving any doctrine from it or the sort of art perpetrated by those cultural freelancers in the rue Vilin (above the rue des Envierges) with their phoney naïve paintings and their pink graffiti. Like them, I would try to arouse public attention to the necessity of dreams as a guarantee of independence, but also to the question of what creates dreams – and how can they be made to disappear? Waste lands of the soul, and Heaven only knows what can happen in them, what ingenuous poets and criminals can slip into them. So to dress up an area of waste land into a nursery playground is to risk offending the very essence of the god's freedom, neglecting the fact that what he teaches, just as much as some obscure hope, is solitude and fear of death. Full stop. I am reading out this speech under my breath in front of the place Falguière, of which there is virtually nothing left. Both sides of the rue d'Alleray sink away into waste ground, but it is my mumbling, not the place itself, that attracts the wary interest of passers-by. When this happens, I usually move off. And besides, I intend to dissolve my movement the minute it starts to take shape. It has even left my mind by the time I have crossed the square to the rue de la Procession. Next comes a bit of the rue de Gergovie (everything is from Gaul around here) and the rue Vercingétorix with further stretches of ruins: as fawning as spaniels, a few condemned trees submerge a flight of twenty steps or so and the iron handrail down to the pavement, and on the right at the back of a blind alley there are houses beneath a froth of tiny white blossoms, as sad and intimidated as the brides in old photos. Meanwhile the scudding sky has become overcast again. I have only two minutes to get to the station. It commands the intersection of the lines from Montparnasse and those of the Petite-Ceinture down

39

in its cutting. The position of this rural station means that beneath it there is a whole maze of underground passages on different levels, as dark as those in a castle.

But I remain seated above on the only bench in the waiting-room, next to the luggage weighing-machine that can seldom be used any more, between alternate gusts of rain and railway coaches.

What is going on? There are shouts ricocheting off the house fronts, not screams of terror, yet there is a wariness in the way that the lights go on in several windows and the outlines of people in nightclothes stir the curtains. And once again these shouted challenges start up, like those in *The Iliad*. I grasp the word *brocanteur*. Perhaps this is how Hector humiliated Achilles before the latter literally hung up his arms like something from a flea market. Leaving these heights of epic poetry, it occurs to me that the secondhand dealer who sometimes comes on his rounds towards ten in the morning has temporarily struck it rich: in which case, like everyone else, he has treated himself to a trip to Bangkok and the jet-lag has played havoc with his sense of time. But what is going on out there has nothing to do with secondhand dealers nor with the brawls of drunks or heroes. I open the window, look out, and down below on the square I see these two fellows raising a racket and at last I grasp the words *pommes de terre*. With their eyes raised upwards, they spot me at once and set upon me immediately: 'Fifteen francs a 25 kilo sack!' I tell them I'm coming. They start bawling away again and use my custom as an example to the entire silent, expectant neighbourhood. I would go down to them even if their potatoes were double the price. I am as moved as if it were Rimbaud flogging old rifles. Business is conducted at speed, without ado. He is a thin young man with a black moustache, hollow eyes drained with fatigue. Half farmworker, half garage mechanic. He comes from an exhausted, heavy sky that floats aimlessly between clover and car engines.

'So where are you from?'
'Normandy.'
'But why from so far away? Why this bother, and so late?'
'Because they treat us all like shit.'

Our eyes meet for a mere second, but it's enough. I hear their lorry start up as I hoist up my sack. By morning they will be near Bourg-Theroulde (pronounced Boutroude) or Bayeux. Parked askew in some ditch, they are able to doze at least, their heads flopped against the windows or wrapped in their arms over the steering-wheel, grey like their spuds, grey like daybreak with its anaesthetic softness.

Between the sooty twirls in a sky disturbed by flushes of pink, I
stop up here near the bridge. The last bridge in Paris to the west,
with piles as thin as razorblades. I can see the dusty city on my
right and on the left, the darker slopes covered only with
boxwood. The hour is midday and it is Sunday, the day when it
is possible to go up one-way streets. So I freewheel back down
the same ramp and punctuate my descent with frequent
snatches of braking. For I intend to float along beneath the
embankment and the long factory buildings with square
wooden towers like those on the forts of the last Merovingian
kings. But at the same time I would have liked to stay by the
depot where VIDAL ET CHAMPREMONDE pile up car bodies
behind the station on the Boulevard-Victor. I like rails, scrap-iron
and rust when the unchanging sky leaps and swells above them.
I turn off at the rue Saint-Charles into the beginnings of a virgin
forest beneath the watery density of plane trees that are never
pruned. I become absorbed in them in the full knowledge that I
absolutely have to go home (something like a joint of veal will be
overcooked otherwise), and it is certain that I am going to return
home, that I have done so. But the person I left behind by the
trees and the scrap iron, on the edge of the bridge, is not willing
to budge one inch; he is fixed there and has understood.

Moving from one place to the next in one of the functions
of my job which sometimes requires me to cart around parcels,
despite the inconvenience I very seldom take the direct route
and so tonight I find myself close to the slope of Chaillot.
Lower down I'll stop for a second by the bust of a poet
and whisper him some stanzas of his Graveyard by the Sea.
This handsome compact head without a memory is exiled here
close to a humble attempt at a waterfall under laurels.
And here my brain meditates in turn: on fate, on fame, on peace.
In the persistent dark bushes forsythias burst forth
and the more vigorously they spring the more distraught they
    seem . . .
After the mildness of March comes the harshness of Easter,
with those rustlings on the marble and a steely sky's gleam.
The sun is hardly more than a mere aspirin tablet
as it dissolves in the fog, and all the monuments
seen to the south of the city from this esplanade —
Les Invalides, Saint-Sulpice, the towers, Notre-Dame, the
    Panthéon —
seem shrivelled, stricken with a slack uncertainty,
ready to merge with the shivering ruins of the houses.
A touch crystallized by cold myself in the middle of the terrace
(and here, with his hand behind his back, casual and very keen
an old man circles skilfully on roller skates).
I check once more the mystery of his civil consecration
– a divine one too – in the winds that swell the air
as they used to swell the souls of our great republicans.
And as I leave these gardens, light flakes of snow
come down and melt on the nose of Valéry, composing a poem
from this bronze and the pink blossom of a Japanese cherry.

From one day to the next between 31 August and 1 September (with the density of the traffic moving from zero to one hundred per cent), most journeys turn into so many suicide attempts. I try in vain to find a way to get from the Rond-Point to Saint-Paul for instance, because I am plunged willy-nilly into a sea of missiles, the most threatening being the taxis of course, since for them every ramshackle two-wheeler like mine represents less of a hindrance than a personal insult. And so they aim straight at me on purpose, and scrape by me in the hope of throwing me off balance and annihilating me beneath the low snouts of buses charging along their lanes in the opposite direction. I know their game. For a long time now I have been thinking of getting a rear-view mirror that would enable me to keep an eye on their little tricks and stave off the aggression of these killers. But if I did this I would run the risk of looking solely to the rear and crashing into the nearest lamp-post. But they know this too, these taxi-drivers. They are up to every trick in the book. In any case, I can still detect them well enough by keeping my ears open for the steady, sly, dull sound of the diesel throbbing away like a tug. The repeated failure of this permanent aggressiveness of theirs is absurd proof of their black designs. In fact I catch up with them anyway every two hundred metres, at the lights, and give them one of my bland inscrutable looks from beneath the peak of my cap. And then they get the message, snort with rage, turn pale, spit at me in their imagination, while I have been known to spit at the door of their cab for real, and then off we go, me and my handy little machine, down a side street. So keep running! It makes me feel like an old lath and canvas Spad, making a getaway after machine-gunning a Zeppelin. But more often than not I have to hold my ground. The other day I battled with one of these horrors all the way from Alma to Raspail. Brooom! Brooom! – at every green light he thought he was going to nail me to the spot and I – without any margin of acceleration power over him, there I am, chug, chug, at the next red light, my marble profile driving him wild again. Yet out of the corner of my eye I noted that he had had enough and that insults were about to wrench themselves from the filth of his entrails, probably the usual *You stupid bugger!* But sorry, I'm wrong. I was dealing with someone with a certain refinement about him, at least someone with the underhand and inventive sense of provocation, a Mediterranean skill that dates back to the Trojan braggarts. Honeyed and vindictive, smiling carnivorously all over his face, he leans out and asks me if I really am the sheriff of Aubervilliers. Not a bad guess, I retort, but I'm merely the Lone Ranger of Saint-Ouen. And since I know that I can make an easy and immediate escape to the left because he is already signalling to the right for his passenger, Wham! – and (conforming to the harsh rules of warfare) I aim a whacking great gob of spit onto his bonnet.

I move along unhurriedly in the softly deepening greyness, walking in the middle of the grass. On either side of me is this dreadful traffic of hurtling cars packed with unreal and empty faces with their eyes set on death; on either side this dreadful din rages and I no longer hear it, it doesn't really exist for me because, one evening, my mind opened up to the silence of Paris, the silence of the sky, of greyness and of the long grass walk beneath the low branches that join, here between the silent river and these illusory car engines. Although it was probably designed by gentlemen of a Positivist persuasion in elegant morning-coats and the tallest of Offenbach hats, this stretch (where the ground dips down imperceptibly in the middle) is in fact a temple inhabited by an extremely unpretentious god. You will be imagining that I am meditating or prostrating myself. This god asks for nothing so excessive. He knows that, like him, we have been deported to this planet and that, conversely, we shall be expelled from it one of these fine days, and this neither delights him nor moves him in any way. Yet he is not in the least indifferent. How can this paradox be justified? It is hard to explain it, and would serve no purpose anyway. Don't let's confuse the god and theology but remain as near as possible, in spirit and in deed, to his silence and his bare simplicity. I could, for instance, have piously removed my shoes before treading on this sacred grass. But in the first place it is rather damp; and then my thick Argyll socks have got big holes at the toes; and finally, the god doesn't give a toss about it, if you will pardon the expression. Likewise, I ought completely to still my mind, but that is not imperative either. The insubstantial presence of this greyness soaks into me, and that is enough. Now guess what I am thinking about in this holy place? – of Marie; of Maria and Marie; of my loves. With leaves of the ivy that used to grow along the embankment wall and which is now dead, ten years ago and in this very spot I made an immortal coronet, and I will not repudiate it. But, in the greatest secrecy, I am making another one for another person and she is at this moment in the sky like an angel (on board a plane). Strong and graceful antelope, noble and most touchy Lady, explosive and silly, and brilliant enough for twelve of her kind, it grieves me that here she is, flying off to some Club Méditerranée with one hundred and thirty silly buggers and here am I, the hundred and thirty first, on the banks of the Seine, tortured by this double vision: up she goes, up she goes, becoming incandescent in the white dress I love so much, clear and breathtaking like the meaning of the world contained in the outbursts of her laughter, yet at the same time my limited gifts of premonition tell me she is snatched up by fate at the end of the runway, thrown into the ancient journey through anguish and tears which she too must travel as a real woman after all, it not being enough for her to remain a goddess or to beat me at running down corridors. But Lord, I commend her to your keeping: may she not suffer too much anxiety in the sky, may nothing or no one crush her, and may I see her eyes again, unharmed, childlike and as golden as the round chestnuts that are tumbling to the ground here (I pick up one or two, or three). Meanwhile here comes the raging chorus of the Erinyes to apostrophize me thus: What have you done with your wife in the face of the strict Sacrament and before the increasingly lax law of men, you bastard? She too deserves, and quite rightly, the sweet name of Marie and you gave it to her – and oh! I feel shame, and bitterness, and love. Stones of the cold stone parapet over the icy water, console me; with your profound tranquillity of a judge weighing up the evidence, bring reassurance to this hypocritical and loose-living Platonist who has had nothing better to do than to cast this pretentious language of love to the winds of his life. And I stumble up against the Pont Alexandre. Or rather the bridge looms up literally out of the void, out of some other nonsensical system of stars, evoked by those spheres, steps, bronzes, lamp-standards, stone blocks, and the majestic roadway where (like Zizi Jeanmaire with a bunch of feathers sticking out of her behind) the Tsarina of Trigamma is going to alight from an interstellar rocket like something out of *Star Wars*. Meanwhile, very slowly, though very quickly in fact, beneath the arch of the bridge, along comes the bow of one of those long barges that are no longer towed but are pushed along from behind; and there are two of them end to end, which makes you wonder what happens when they get to locks or to bends in the river. But the strangest thing of all seems to be the load they carry: as if a whole by-road undergoing maintenance work had been transferred just like that onto these barges, with stones, rabbit grass and heavy marl and, in the increasingly dense greyness that does not hinder his work in the least, the divine roadmender digging away with his pickaxe and not even about to turn his head as he sails past the Eiffel Tower.

What too many people are apt to forget, the delivery man confides to me, is that when it comes down to it, we are just passengers in this world, and for a really short time. So that everything happens the wrong way round: hate all over the place where there ought to be love. Such are the words he addresses to me in a tongue as hard to reproduce as his accent: pure Parisian with a sort of haughty assurance peeping out from the cocky humour. Quite how we got round to this topic, I have no idea: because the lights on the avenue de Suffren are stuck on red, and this traffic holdup is the sort of thing that encourages meditative reflection. I suppose he is on his way to deliver something and that he imagines the same of me: the large carton held in place by a luggage strap behind my saddle (in which I am, in fact, transporting letters, rough drafts, elastic bands and expensive records of Sonny Clark and Eddie Costa), the cap pulled down over my rather tough-looking face, and my anorak with its three white stripes down the sleeves. And it's true that in some ways we are alike, and not simply through the way we are dressed. But I give no more than a serious nod of approval; I don't take the risk of opening my mouth. If I had been the one to come out with a mere third of this burgeoning gospel talk, I am sure he would immediately have treated me like a right little priest. Yet this is what he is turning over in his mind while he waits at the lights or edges forward, and I think about such things too at times. So perhaps for a second, unknown to each other, but elbow to elbow in the unfriendly mingling of traffic, we love and understand one another. But finally the orange light flickers onto the whole crossroad: he re-enters the fray, skips lanes, shakes me off, then suddenly looks back and (let's get the words right) really splits his face from ear to ear with a big smile.

There is something astonishing in the sound of a human voice when you happen to arrive at this little scene, beautifully painted and set back to create the same huge and lofty impression as a stage-set, with no one around, as in a theatre before the play starts – or long afterwards in the night when the play is over and the wordless depths of the drama might surge up into the mind: unimaginable characters, as yet absent from everything else as they are from themselves and whose fate will be decided in perplexed comings and goings, not in words: entrances, exits, enigmatic gestures and stances, immediately followed by growing feverishness and movement. Then suddenly someone starts to speak, and it so happens that the someone is in fact myself. I have come to this place through a series of dark theatre wings, from the Parc Montsouris to the Poterne des Peupliers bridge, simply to buy the stamps I have been asked to get and to use the opportunity as an excuse to revisit the former Petite-Ceinture railway station and the iron footbridge further on, both of them now demolished, and despite the remaining relics of railway activity (an open space, rails, cylindrical drums, carriages) I feel both saddened and plunged into the unexpected once more. Plunged not into the further impressions of a melancholy walker, but – at the end of the rue du Docteur-Landouzy where it meets the rue du Docteur-Leray – into this deserted stage-set of a block of maisonettes, all of them alike, vaguely English in Style, and apparently made of plywood, a touch too peaceful for them not to be hatching some threat (all those doors that could open), a scene where I am obliged to remember exactly something that I none the less have to improvize. For I did know but I have forgotten, because each footstep echoes in the changing future and past of a plot where destinies will be fulfilled. I had better reflect; so that I can at least get a thorough sense of the indications provided by the décor – deserted I repeat, and we go on stage in only a minute's time, but perhaps we never will if the other characters go on hiding – and I find that this décor conforms very well to the truth of the theatre, by which I mean that it exhibits the problematic depths of things that are normally seen as unreal. So much does it conform in fact, that real false memories reoccur to me through contamination: a bicycle shop on the corner of the rue Damesne in which I spent my childhood amid the smell of solder and fresh rubber, then the two shop windows where I start making an endless inventory of the contents, from newspapers to haberdashery by way of a whole mixed bag of cheap goods – liquorice, toys, scent, knick-knacks that you only ever see now in these caverns, and the sight of which made every kid think that one evening he was holding a sixpenny Aladdin's lamp. There is no lack of foodstores here either: fine wines, generous cuts of meat at the back of butchers' shops giving onto the black, icy air. But customers are rare, silent and motionless more than undecided. Why? And the same is true of the shop assistants, cramped up into their shop-coats as if they were waiting for the play to really begin. But is the decision up to me? The rue Dieulafoy that I am following behind this stage-set gives me no enlightenment on the matter. In fact this street is well positioned to hide the scenery supports and between them the secret of the plot with its mass of dumb protagonists. But no. Identical flat and pointed little houses stand there opposite, huddled together, once again implying that there is something hidden behind them, and the only glimmer of light I find comes out of a bush: five yellow roses left by December in eternal bloom. At last, on the other side of the place de l'Abbé-Georges-Hénocque, I catch sight of a *tabac*. The people at the counter and in the wood-panelled café are hardly stirring, and not talking. A young man with a moustache studies me over the till. Yet another person waiting for something to happen. And then my voice, amid so many silences, resonates with the furtive oddity of the first lines. Yet my words contain nothing out of the ordinary: *Have you got any sixty-centime stamps?* But since this is the purpose of my errand, it is true that after a pause I add: *I need a hundred of them,* and that this exactitude supplies the note of a drama about to commence. My role played out, I make off towards the rue de Tolbiac.

Each of these streets is more dismally amnesiac than the next despite their names, which do have memories – the rue de la Fontaine-au-Roi, the rue de la Pierre-Levée, the rue du Moulin-Joli – but up they rise and up I follow. A courtyard, no, an *impasse* lit up by a tree, holds my attention, but it is not curiosity that drives me on past the black wooden house fronts. I respond to whatever it is that batters away behind the nailed doors, to the fiery light in the trees or perhaps to both at once. As if I now finally needed to decide between them. But I have already fallen into the old trap: the illusion that some fated event is still not without hope and repeats itself out of kindness, and there I stand, just on the edge, between the turning beam of light and the darkness doomed to extinction. I stand completely still. I have the feeling that the distracted sky above the rue des Couronnes is about to make the decision for me. Then, several times, someone shouts out *Mohammed, Mohammed* in a thick voice – and almost immediately behind the fluttering sheets of washing, five or six windows half open, then shut at once: our Mohammed is not to be found, everyone is looking for him.

That unfindable something

Sunday morning: like so many others who are Sunday painters, I am becoming a Sunday poet since this is the only day you can work from nature undisturbed. On Saturdays you are snatched up and stupefied by the crowds of people stocking up with provisions for the inevitable tomorrow; all sorts of lovely goodies you simply have to have. Here is the list:–

1. Rue de la Banque. Six bottles of ordinary red wine, and it is not for nothing that for years I have frequently gone to buy my wine so far from where I live. For where I go, behind a rampart of jars of mustard and towering piles of loose sweets, there is a person of immense culture and unerring taste whose kindness and honesty are truly angelic. Here on earth among us, in a single emaciated being with a thin moustache, is the triple incarnation (as far as plonk is concerned) of Thomas Aquinas, Saint François de Sales and Francis of Assisi. In a high dreamy tone, he ponders, makes suggestions and holds forth, finding his way into all the hidden corners of your drinker's soul and illuminating it with his mercy and his wisdom. And while I am always loathe to cart along my empties, I none the less pay the deposit on the bottle with a limpid heart, in an angelic spirit. (19,20F)

2. Rue Saint-Honoré. Three packets of *Leduc* cigarettes from *La Civette*. In my way, I have a fairly unusual and extensive knowledge of tobacco. For years I was a timorous housebound creature whose only reason for leaving the house was to go and buy cigarettes. I am constantly to be seen taking the most unlikely brands from my every pocket, and it will come to the point where I know how to cough in many languages, but few people can bring themselves round to the fact that this is my way of seeking for the Absolute. To me it is instructive and a matter of great beauty that, like everything else, the Absolute should go up in smoke. But I've still not found it. Just a few fair

55

approximations of it like these *Leduc* cigarettes, which are to dark tobacco what British *Capstan Full Strength* are to Virginia, or in another field, what ordinary Luxembourgeois tobacco is to Maryland. This is not the place for private theories about the tobacco products of Turkey, the Canary Islands, Java, the Philippines or certain Cuban mixtures. My *Leduc* cigarettes, quite modestly, come from Belgium, or even the Belgian back of beyond if you like, since nobody had heard of them in Brussels. So I imagine that they must be imported (if not made) just for me these days since I am repeatedly told that I am the only one who buys them. In fact I normally buy them at the drugstore on the Rond-Point, where they have turned me into a celebrity amongst the giggling ladies there who also fail to recognize my quest for the Absolute, because I can't help looking down the cleavage of the one called Joëlle – Joëlle with eyes as grey as the rain on the bright depravity of the sea. (6F)

3. The Quai Voltaire. Three pencils with a special evanescent shade of pink, beige and grey. There are normally far too many people in the shop for me to keep to the following strict rule: make sure you don't linger about and lose your bearings amid pots of gouache, pans of watercolour and the soaring flights of heavenly Ingres or Canson paper. The first sign of straying from the rules comes as I am queuing up at the till: my pencils are joined by a goose-quill that I shall put to even less use. Come on! It's time to get out of here! (7,90F)

4. The rue du Bac. Two school exercise-books with single lines (I have a long-standing hatred of close-lined paper with vertical columns since secondary school) so that I can set down nice regular lines of verse of the kind I no longer write, but with the thought at the back of my mind that some Angel prepared further and even better ones for me, in invisible ink, and that all I shall need to do is to shed a genuine tear onto the paper – (that says a lot). (4,90F)

5. Boulevard Raspail. One more copy of Jaccottet's collection *Leçons*, humble, terrifying and very lofty poetry (there's a leaf to be taken out of this book), and yet another copy of that other

masterpiece by Cingria. What do I do with all these books? I re-read them and then hand them out right and left to people I think they will really impress and who say 'Ah. . .' Mysterious, isn't it? (17F)

6. I only need to cross the road to go into the tiny dairy in the rue de Grenelle, still thinking about Cingria and, by association, of Follain, who one day unnerved the staff of the *Charpentiers* restaurant by punctuating his account of Charles-Albert's death with sobs worthy of the soft-hearted Ajax. It was really impossible to console him and I had to take his hands in mine like a small child's, while he went on spilling half his rum (a ritual of his) as well as his tears all over his star-studded embroidered waistcoat. It was the same day, I think, that with his head in the clouds on some pavement where I was trying to keep him, he told me all about his hatred of those criminal motor cars that force one to *pay attention*. Now attention, he said, was death to the activity of idly strolling about, but in the end this childlike lyrical persistence of his in wandering aimlessly about the place would have been the death of him. He was matchless, was Follain, on all sorts of subjects. Besides poetry, there were things to do with the Church (jargon, liturgy, vestments), there were the cheeses, some of which he would eat on the tip of his knife after energetically mashing them up with plenty of butter. This would provide me with the opportunity of asking him, out of pure mischief, just how much he really liked strong cheeses. But instead of deigning to argue about it, he would aim his dented profile away from such youthful bumptiousness and, speaking at the top of his voice, would broadcast my lamentable lack of enthusiasm for Gris de Lille to all and sundry. From the beautiful and impeccable young woman whose hair and skin are imbued with a host of disturbing smells, I buy a piece of Brie and then half a Gris de Lille in memory of Follain. (12,15F)

7. The rue du Vieux-Colombier. An infantry drummer in a pre-First World War uniform, navy-blue tunic and steel-grey trousers. I suggest, with some confidence, that this is a lucky find, but this saleswoman who has grown constantly younger

over a period of twenty years (she was at least fifty when I started coming here) immediately dashes my spirits, as she usually does, with the information that the figure's half-round modelling is now only of interest to penniless people like me, that there will always be enough of them for the likes of us, and plenty enough, if I need, to reconstitute the thirty battalions with the complete military band at the head. In this cavernous shop where the most ancient dreams prowl about (wonders hidden in drawers, boxes and compartments at the back of cupboards; subdued lighting, dust, the equivocal glances of the fairy or the castrating witch who makes no secret of her horror of lead soldiers), you sometimes run into Grosjean and his Prussian obsessions. And there we are, the two of us, bowing and scraping to each other in greeting like pendulums, nearly knocking our heads together, so delightful is it to meet up again for real in this dream world. Besides, this is how I think Grosjean needs to be understood, since he himself is like a metaphorical character out of a dream, an imperial and lunar bird of prey from the deserts of Frederick, Mahomet and Solomon. I fail to grasp his theories, it is true, but not the coherence of their never-ending palaver, which the angelus is loathe to interrupt as it ripples in sheets of liquid gold from the towers of Saint-Sulpice. (18F)

8. The rue de Rennes. A Bud Powell record reissued by a Japanese company. Not that I shall listen to it this evening, and probably not even tomorrow. I will save it for a time when I feel, rightly or wrongly, that I have a right to such pathos, and when I need to remind myself just how much a man can be innocent and crushed (I am thinking of Bud's *It never entered my mind*, so close, in the way if falters in the face of dire extremity, to the chorale *Erbarm' dich mein* or, if it comes to that, to Jaccottet's *Leçons*) and yet how he can cling on, even in such straights, to blind hope. But that's enough of that. Apart from this Powell record, which seems to me to be a must, there is plenty in the display racks to keep you in torture for hours or bankrupt you in one swoop. When it comes to making a choice, I am so

undecided that I make my selection out of a kind of rivalry: I think about Berg and wonder whether he, a real wild boar from the Vosges with his sense of scent and his readiness to pounce, has already sniffed out this Bill Perkins for instance. In fact what a pleasure it would be, were we to speak on the 'phone, to introduce some apparently casual aside like 'By the way, I've found this Bill Perkins, you know the one I mean, *Octette*; it's not bad at all.' I can hear Berg now, struggling like a wild boar to stop himself choking with rage, and I can imagine his next move. In the time it takes to replace the receiver, in a single leap he will jump clear of all his drum-kit clobber and his twelve metres of balcony, casting a huge hooked-nosed Saxony shadow against the wall where I intend one day to go and paint the famous 'blue line of the Vosges' for him, complete with fir trees, Schlucht and the Ballon d'Alsace peak. Luckily, Berg lives on the third floor, and will land unharmed on the opposite side of the street beneath a shop sign that can be read as *Ti-Jean* if, like Berg and myself, you are crazy about Kerouac (and West Coast jazz, and Bud, and the hundreds of others). (43F)

9. The rue Saint-Placide. The sheet music of a recorder piece by Jean-Baptiste Loeillet. As if by chance, this sonata is on display in the window. Far from simplifying matters, this complicates them dramatically. As it happens, a wooden partition like a church stall separates the display window from the austere shop at mid-height (it is somewhat like being inside a Balzacian solicitor's office in Coutances rather than a ten-minute walk away from the Tour Montparnasse or Saint-Germain-des-Prés). In order to reach the music they have somehow managed to place on display, these old ladies, who are not exactly bending over backwards to be pleasant, have first to perch themselves on a little bench, then to lean over and flail about in space, as best they can. So here am I, looking at a high-wire act that is scaring me to death, with this unfortunate balancing rod suddenly in rigid but precarious balance on the narrow edge of the knife-like partition, exactly like a pair of scales hovering between two roughly equal weights, but in this instance the weight of her

head is threatening to tip over and with it the rest of the lady, neck of the thighbone and all, into biographies of César Franck and manuals on the rudiments of music. Acutely aware of the urgent necessity of coming to her aid, I make a split-second calculation that it would take far too long to get round the polished counter, too wide for me to straddle, so that, amid general stupefaction, I climb onto it just in time to give a discreetly helping hand to the heavily-clad feet of the victim and miraculously bring them down again onto the little bench. I descend from the counter with my face almost as red as it would be if I had forgotten to do up my flies, and try to divert attention by polishing the counter with my sleeve and presenting the old ladies with my compliments on their old typewriter: it's a 1930 Underwood, spick and span, towering up like Manhattan, beautifully maintained, with the same newness about it that it must have had the moment when Andy Razaf finished using it to type the words of *My fate is in your hand* (and you can say that again!) for Fats Waller. (13,50F)

10. I am sorry to inform the reader that there will be no money spent in this tenth section. I was counting on putting a modest two francs' worth of two-stroke mixture in my tank at the petrol pump in the rue de Sèvres, and not for the first time I discover that this pump, and the next, are out of order. And so from one pump to another, I arrive in the depths of the fifteenth *arrondissement* as evening falls, and with it my consumer extravagance. And immediately, in self-punishment, I get a miserly whim into my head which means that my petrol tank dries up and I am forced to pedal. Pay, I say to myself, pay now, you cretin, with the sweat of your brow for these sybaritic pranks of yours, when your family is without shoes, lipstick or meat. And I drip with sweat all the way along the merciless walls of the rue Leblanc and on the rise that goes up to the Garigliano bridge. But, as often on my wanderings, my mind gets carried away and loses sight of the penitential nature of this journey. On the other side of the boulevard I am crossing is a long avenue with small aspen trees and large cobblestones. It

beckons me so tenderly into its sloping bend and I turn into it. First I see a man with two small girls looking for some unfindable thing or other in the humdrum grass on the side of the road, then three or four cars pass by furiously flashing their headlights to make me realize I am going up a one-way street. Drive on, I shout at them, drive on, you heap of anathema; make the air stink, block the ring roads, you will not stop the wind, which already smells of snow and wolf's fur, from blowing, nor the moon, half-drunk already, but with all its wits about it, from coursing along ahead of this orgy of celestial grape harvest above Meudon and Saint-Cloud. A few metres more and I stop. I go through some boards and into a building site: a huge excavation with an emerald and purple Dead Sea, and a gigantic mountain of rubble above it. I climb to the top and sink in thigh deep. If the whole thing collapsed, when and in what state would they discover me, in this mass of plaster and wooden beams? I am frightened, I don't dare move about too much. Eventually I gently disengage my leg and test out the surface around me: it is firm, and down below I can hear the reassuring metal clanking of a train. The Versailles line. Hello there, you good people, and I hail them with much waving of my cap. No one responds. They are all off back to their suburbs, encumbered and, like me, bewildered by their parcels of shopping. So are we all this much alike in our solitude; so much crass frenzy, so little love, merely this sullen gloom that portends the wretchedness of Sunday deep in our hearts? Gradually silence comes and the kindness of night. Like a disappointed barbarian I remain huddled on my mound, with my back to the ruins of Paris.

A little blue door

And then even it has shed its flowers, the tall plant in the rubble
seen stooping again in October above walls
and whose name I did not know – bare stem with clusters of the
    palest mauve flowers
at home near plaster (calcicolus, I am told),
the final and quite feeble effort that the season makes
to stop things sinking into colourless indifference
poker-faced, as the expression goes – as if
a flower could smile or scowl at every act of cruelty
plant-like or human that is done without thinking
in the rubble of love's flesh and lime.
Where is it gone –
the time I imagined myself moved by the sadness of buddleias
an amateur hiker certain of his return to a warm house
to write up his polished little virtuoso piece
with the pat expression and well-placed moments of lyrical
intensity and quibbling use of comma? I in turn
am bent against the wall, tossed by the charging wind
like someone pacing the same path in distress, yet with nothing
more to do now at the end of this street – the rue Lecourbe
once again and then comes the rue de la Convention,
with each new house alike coldly uninhabited
though one, or several, ladies go inside with flowers,
puffing on the creaking stairway, in the choking lift,
their one free hand restoring a touch of bouffant to their hair.
As the door opens dark and cold like an aged mouth
I hear Widow Eternity rambling on in the drawing-room
beyond a string of scrap iron bridges trembling, trembling –
then comes the endless end, the final dismay
of abomination, of shit-hole desolation,
whistling November wind and flowers for my hollow bones.

What kind of hope is left in the face of those evenings when nothing shows resistance any more: neither bridges nor tower-blocks, women nor clouds, nothing, not even a lyrical inclination towards amazement or lament, because that is what you wished for – to merge with the deadened air and all this unfeeling concrete. (Yet no. One knows that this feeling of squashed resistance comes about through the power of another consistently methodical will, principally when love and anger are in conflict with each other; through a spectre with a remotely human form – the clothes and gestures, the glances and the words that pass judgement and lay down the law – to create the illusion that its behaviour matches human behaviour; and this spectre leaves you free to speak out while silently repudiating all that you say; and should you feel queasy it prescribes the exact dose of poison in the guise of money, tranquillizers, shame and vitamins. With your head held high, you affirm how right it is and it allows such a show of pride, even requires it of you; it relishes the dulled pride which at the very most is liable to dry up in bitterness when you go scowling alone beneath the trees as darkness falls and you no longer notice it nor see the trees or the sky which was able to offer you an escape from the imprisoning circle of this state willed upon you and which shows you, to no avail, houses, bridges, clouds, people and people like you who are no longer capable of a crime or a tear.)

The shadow moves up over the Butte-aux-Cailles. But a single sliver of glass or jade illuminates the horizon and on it the clouds place a wall that by some miracle stays standing. As ever I am reminded of the lower part of a forehead crossed by some deep thought. Already two stars gaze intently in the gap. It is damp and cold. Over towards the place d'Italie the sky is quite different, with pink and blue pastel strokes amid the rust of lithographic trees. I leave the rue de Tolbiac. And there before me, straight away, in the rue Moulin-des-Prés, the first light of evening (as you'd say the first light of dawn) slips into the scene, and it could be an evening of rioting because I feel high up and cut off, familiar with the maze (the rue Samson, the rue Jonas) in which the stream of silhouetted figures suggests a dense cluster of the common people – and in this area that is still conceivable – clinging furtively together out of stubbornness. The only thing that is missing perhaps is their weapons. They will be found. Enough to hold out for a few days beneath the already crumbling house fronts (in the rue Vandrezanne and the passage Boiton) and without having to defend any cause: merely this fury, like the icy sky there in the distance, burning the forests of cranes to ashes.

I do, among a lot of fascinating but useless objects, none the less possess a knapsack, a laburnum stick and a sturdy pair of shoes. So what on earth am I doing here in the rue La Boétie, brimming with white wine and exalted thoughts of Being and The Void? Wondering what weird kind of music our words have produced for the god who has commanded us to be watchful; when without awaiting or fearing any particular time, the least of the stones of this earth is watchful about breaking in half in the night. Any stone you like, and, balancing on it, the only edifice of its kind, without arches, porch or pillar. On the other side of the street, some distance away by now, I can see my pal turn round with a final wave of his arm, and one of those looks of a man hatching a plot that ends up conveying the message 'They won't get us'. For this street with its appearance of tranquillity is utterly repressive: straight, empty and as bloodchilling as its street-lamps that do nothing to dissipate the darkness. It would be preferable to be a mere knapsack and pair of shoes on the road, but that is not possible. The only thing incumbent on me here is to remain patient, hypocritical and ordinary, and to parade a sour-tempered or a placid expression in order to keep my distance. Yet I am delighted to have understood something and understood it thoroughly. What? Even if I knew, I would certainly not tell. Anyway, it's a secret. Many of those who know it are unaware that they share it, but that is part and parcel of it: this watchful humility of being unaware, the love that is more resolute than refusal, and no stick or knapsack between the asphalt and the gentle rain in which I walk, unassailable.

I am bringing back some home-made *pâté de campagne* from the
Butte-aux-Cailles; the *charcutière* complained of the heat. Yet you
can feel the humidity and the cool in the depths of the air as you
ride along, a breath of all this water. For in May, Paris becomes
an entirely aquatic city; in the hollows and on the heights there is
the same liquid texture, scarcely less dense in the depths of
impasse and courtyard, around the street-lamp in the passage
Vandrezanne, in the accumulating masses of underwater greenery amid which the rue Bobillot floats and threads its way. So
how can you remain for more than five minutes on the tracks of
the Petite-Ceinture which can be reached over a demolition
ramp in the rue Gazan? I dread being stifled or devoured in this
railway cutting. Tigers and boas are rife in the raging thickets on
the embankment. I go up again and back towards the Butte:
through the place Paul-Verlaine and the rue des Cinq-Diamants.
Through the dense air people call out to their kids to come
home, wash and eat; that will take a long time. The calls come
down from an inhabited cliff-face erected in a half circle with
identical niches in it, in front of a broad stretch of bare ground
that deliberately refuses to turn green. Close to half-roasted
thuyas a dozen sickly birch trees are dying. They should simply
have left the anarchic seeds from building sites to grow here; this
desert would not be what it is now, a forest star-studded with tin
cans and phosphorescent eyes. It has the advantage of being laid
out like a theatre and I am the only person in the audience. But
although I am standing still and wordless in the middle of the
stage, I am certainly an object of spectacle myself for the many
eyes hidden behind the reflections of pane-glass doors. Every
now and again one of these doors opens and, whatever the floor
level, the story always begins with a young woman with a
watering can. And while she moistens her flowers, behind her
you can glimpse a section of lacquered kitchen or the softened

66

corner of a bedroom, the place where life begins, and so from there a thousand lives which tangle into infinite meshes of bifurcations, interconnections between circuits of emotion and thought, irradiating the whole vibrant city beneath its weight of water. And now the children are coming home and I pick out their names (Elodie, Cédric, Géraud), which are slightly snobbish for such a district. Their faces are the faces of dazzled, furious savages, and they are still dragging their heels, moving off and lingering at the other end of the flat space, tiny figures amid the towering letters of the word SUZE positioned above the Cité des Artistes.

A froth of acacia blossom hangs above the pavement. I can only see three young ladies who might want to pick clusters of them: they will not be able to reach. I'd find it natural enough to come to their assistance, but what would they think, and then what about me as I perform an unsteady leg up? So I wait for them to disappear before I plunge my arms into the bubbling cool milk of these giants of the Petite-Ceinture. The blossoms smell like haylofts from a summer of raining downpours (I remember the summer of '43), like *Senior Service* cigarettes, the neck of a young girl and camomile – in short, they smell first and foremost like acacias. They are so innocently white, so fragile, that I fill my saddlebag with some reluctance: the elastic strap is going to snap in the rue d'Alésia and get tangled up in the chain, and this will add prosaic complications to the rest of the day, when what I had in mind was to change my life drastically by offering these flowers . . . but I digress, or more particularly, I anticipate: I haven't even reached the corner of the rue de Patay near the *Pente douce* restaurant; I am still only starting on the descent towards the last hanging kitchen gardens of the rue Regnault, and there it is *in the misty distance of a dreamed-of Africa*, of horizons photo-engraved like a geography atlas, absurd but inevitable, nameless, senseless, useless, that fresh-blown fragment of the absolute, the mountain peak in the Vincennes zoo.

To the north, between the place des Alpes and the mysterious Yéo-Thomas, the rue du Château-des-Rentiers starts to near its end. They are demolishing the *Café Bouchard*. By contrast, in the rue du Dessous-des-Berges, some plate-glass Anglo-Japanese highriser has just been erected, a building conceivable perhaps in Brussels, but not here. This inconsistency goads me into a quick about-turn in the direction of Masséna, a humming slope where, before I reach the Pont National, I inspect that station which seemed disused to me at first, with absolutely no means of entry alongside a flood of railway lines submerging the canalized dribble of the Seine. I was completely wrong. There is a means of entry and one that appeals to me: down a flight of stairs and through a subway that leads down to the other side of the Ceinture, in front of a building with some pretensions of officialdom about it; it stands there sheer with its seven large dusty bays, and the words CHEMIN DE FER inscribed upon it. The inscription is not without its point, for though it is easy to see that this is a station from the boulevard, from the rue Regnault you would just as easily take it for a town hall, the one like the other transplanted into a still almost visible setting of rhododendrons and fir trees. Inside, the walls have been freshly repainted in ochre, and the ceiling is a soft midnight blue. The voluminous stairwell has plenty of room to spread itself, and from step to step you get the impression you are going down, even though you are going up. There is a silence like the silence that falls in the evening over some wedding in the provinces, in a Village Hall, the only people left being a couple of half-dazed kids beneath the benches. Up near the ticket offices a footbridge enables you to reach those platforms still in use, shaken by trains from Spain, Arpajon and Orléans. I am going back over the bridge now: it seems that at night the police use it to rehouse the drunken tramps who have been turned out of the Métro (I had this from one of them while I was helping him to cobble together his pushcart). Over on the other side I reach the Pont de Tolbiac, in the rue de Dijon amid the farm buildings of Bercy that roll off in waves beneath their never-ending rooftops weighed down with age-old moss. Above them, the most poetic trees in the entire city form an arch and, beneath it, far away but quite clearly outlined in the sand by a moonbeam, is inscribed the neo-Greek pediment of the Nativity Church, pious and humble.

After missing my train, I walk around Saint-Lazare: the rue de Rome, the rue de Vienne, the rue de Londres, the rue d'Amsterdam. It is eight o'clock. After the hysteria of crowds sucked up towards twenty-six platforms, the calm footsteps of stupefaction spread themselves comfortably once more, and the eye of the Great Empty Head opens again. I would be quite unable to assert that it is still daylight or that darkness had already fallen, given that I always see this district as drenched in a kind of transparency, of lighting that has nothing to do with stars or sun. It is almost the same abstract glimmer of a dream, but there is an impeccable nullity here that makes its presence felt in solid shapes; the respectability of the fronts of buildings, the propriety of the pavements, of the cafés swept clean beneath their seats, and the seats themselves seem extremely pleased to be stacked up. In all, a cooperative nullity, attentive to small details like these box trees or the privets that great cross-sections of buildings allow to grow in curly triangles in a garden. At the corner of the rue de Léningrad and the rue de Liège this garden is quite enough decoration, thank you very much. Everything else marks out the strictly defined boundary where, despite certain vague desires for something with a solid presence, held in check by so much coldness, an exchange does take place between what is quite tangibly there and what, no less tangibly, just doesn't exist. So there might just as well be nothing here, it would be much easier – and certainly less painful – but what is in fact quite apparent is that the presence of things is necessary (houses, privets, myself) for the nullity to attain the impeccable heights of its pure loss. And against this *trompe-l'œil* dividing two absences of depth, it is easy to see that the only acceptable halo of plenitude should have been the pink lamp of Mallarmé's cigar. Yes, a pink lamp I would say, as I leave the rue de Rome for a second time to go and look at the railway tracks beneath the Pont de l'Europe gleaming in an yx pattern, bevelled like a crystalline sonnet. And I come down again through the rue d'Amsterdam towards the brasserie where people stand gulping down revolting bowls of mussels, my favourite stopping-point in the past when I had already developed the habit of missing trains, and where, in order to blot themselves out in an embrace, two masses of darkness would seek each other out right through me, paring me down to the thinness of a barely misted window, in the *Café Fleur*.

Since the blowlamp attack on the Citroën depots, very few of the entrances were functioning on the right-hand side of this street (and they are all locked up like safes at the Compressed Air works), whereas on the left, a single entrance, and a rather mysterious one, suggested the existence of a tunnel under the embankment. The result was that, apart from the odd car hurtling from Balard to the Boulevard Périphérique, excited by the idea of this short cut, no one thought of coming down here in the evening or on Sundays, even less of stopping. So I was sure that I would be able to commune with my thoughts in the utmost tranquillity, seated on the pavement with my back against a wall, with another wall opposite. All that could be seen above this second wall were emblems of the railway: the roof of a Métro carriage, the red and white chequered pattern on signal boards like the insignia of the Polish Air Force and, as always, the rough pale aristocratic grass on the embankment. Gusts of warm wind swept down between the two walls. It bore the mingled smells of plaster, solder and red-hot metal from the depots, and then the far from ruffled cohesion of a small body of bits of paper. Not once did they stop rustling together, waffling on, organizing races, voting almost unanimously on motions made with raised hand, or – and this fascinated me most of all – forming two large ritual circles whirling around faster and faster, in opposite but concentric directions, gradually reducing space to an empty centre in which one piece of paper, a prey to sudden inspiration, leaping out of the circling motion, came and danced, soon to be caught up again in the whirlwind of circles that ended up merging into one, spreading out in a sluggish swirl over which the next inspired piece of paper (at first bent on timid attempts at levitation) flew off, orbiting in a series of extremely graceful and skilled figures – turns in every direction, hesitation flick-rolls, doing the falling leaf, divebombing – before coming down to land again, not without a touch of showing off, amid the applause of the asphalt. Then, until the next gust of wind, this paper encampment quietened down. I could once again turn my undivided attention to the calm wall opposite and the waves of clouds in transit towards the north-east. And as a bright patch slowly made its appearance in the greyness – light gold, then soft blue, and finally the crazy white of an oxyhydrogen flame – I too broke out into the laughter of a sainted fool.

The thing that pleases me about the rue des Pyrénées is first of all the fact that it rises and bends in a series of sections that seem to run in a straight line on the map, but in fact form part of an enormous circular arc that goes from the Porte de Vincennes to Belleville by way of Ménilmontant. On the flat of the place Gambetta you take it for granted that this street comes to an end but, showing no sign of fatigue, off it goes again, more sprightly even than it was before, swaying around among the acacia trees. The second attraction is these trembling trees. Plane trees or chestnuts would be less in keeping here, better suited to preserve the quietness of an esplanade or the balance of a lopsided garden square, whereas this prolonged shiver melts into the quivering altitude and helps the sky to trickle down through the branches onto the pavement. In fact there is a square, a hidden one, overlooking the street and accessible by a flight of steps screened by the bushes growing on the slope. Closed off on the other side by the south-west corner of the Père-Lachaise cemetery and very well protected on all sides by its high position as well, its lay-out suggests something of a sense of initiation. This is obviously not deliberate, but that makes it all the more apparent towards midday when the square is deserted, apart from the little yellow lorry left by a kid on the bench where I am sitting. And so it is that my occasional pauses in such places initiate me, but into what I couldn't exactly say. For I certainly don't succumb to ecstasy, nor do I meditate. I hover there in a sort of stupor. There comes a moment when my still lucid gaze deserts me, no longer joined in any way to this completely hazy body, but open to the denser space that draws it in and will reveal to me from outside what rank I occupy in its wisdom. In fact I feel I am being gazed at too intently. It is time to go, but not before replacing the little yellow lorry I was absentmindedly twiddling in my hand and whose owner (he came back while I was deep in my trance) was wondering how he could get it back from this loony adult.

These wonderful Sunday mornings with no honking cars, this wonderful chalky light in which the smallest detail is set, are all I could wish for. I set out to see something new but, falling into my old habits, I end up once again in the rue Leblanc. Yet in less than three weeks everything has changed, and if this is not true of the railway embankment it is, I notice, of most of the Citroën factory buildings opposite. And all that is left standing of the one over there is a high section of arched brick wall with six windows plumb in the centre, the grill they form bringing the sky nearer: the very fact that these window-bars interpose a frame and a prohibitive barrier creates the impression that what shows through them could be accessible – and what you can see through them is the peacefulness of this soft grey, which blends so well with the clumps of pallid urban grass over there, and those gleaming ears of corn, the rail tracks on the Quai de Javel. Running along this railway line there is just one fence, which has become symbolic, and there is no one about to shout me off. And even if a train driver on the Invalides–Versailles branch line sends warning signals to me from his last stop, at the speed his heavy engine shambles along I have all the time in the world to create a little samba routine on the sleepers before I have to get off the track, pausing only to examine the mechanism of the points – ingenious but assembled with a sort of makeshift, common touch about it – and then to reassure myself that there is nothing coming up behind me, for instance, an unexpected train, rapid and silent, which could catch up with me on the bend where, beneath the bridge, the line slips off peacefully towards the hills. You have to watch out for these things. I remember only too well the day a whole ceiling nearly collapsed on my head in a deceptively peaceful lounge in the old Iéna hotel. I climb back over the fence. And I do so for another reason: I thought I'd seen the door of one of the workshops ajar.

The watchmen at the Citroën factory can be accused of many things, but not of lack of vigilance. What this means is that tomorrow at the latest the inexorable advance of the funereal Front de Seine luxury blocks is going to crush all this to the ground. I go into this nave of a place and start calling out *Ho! ho!* The echo immediately bestows on me the stereophonic favour of the one distinct but disappointing reply of which the Unknown judges me worthy: the sound of my own voice, circling around in this condemned hotchpotch of joists and girders. And I think of the many men who have not even finished submitting to whatever hard job of work it may have been under this roof, because they have to go and find work again somewhere else. And perhaps we ought to preserve some of these sanctuaries, to make people understand or to scare them, when they walk about feeling that it can't happen to them, on a Sunday, beneath the freedom of the sky.

It is common knowledge that the former station in the rue de Boulainvilliers is occupied by a lady dentist, but does it actually belong to her? There is another nameplate, for a shooting-gallery, on the railings a bit further along, and I become absorbed in making possible connections between the two. Never have I heard the whir of a dentist's drill in this place, nor the sound of rifles going off; perhaps it all happens in the darkness of the railway tunnels. A bridge straddles the tracks behind the railway building and extends it by adding a glass gallery that looks like a greenhouse set in the depths of a park. But at certain times in the evening it reminds me of the superstructure of a ship, and this blending of railway and sea bang in the middle of the sixteenth *arrondissement* is somehow gratifying. I ended up imagining this place decked out with ship's rope and brass lamps, transformed into a bar given over exclusively to heavy Irish beers and treacly port wine. Mere literary exoticism of course, outmoded and facile, but quite deliberate. The club would be called *Le Barnabooth*. Social climbers and well-heeled but nostalgic literary gentlemen would come here to commune with their thoughts. From time to time a train would be made to go by with a real engine (I mean a steam one) and the journey could proceed in a Pullman as far as the Seine, where passengers would be transferred to a real little steamship (I mean one with funnels) for a cruise to the Pont Mirabeau or to the Institute. It would perhaps be lucrative to refine on this by inventing (like Larbaud and indeed like everyone else at a certain point of their lives) a special nationality with its own flag, rubber stamp and passport, and above all, heavy tax duties. Obviously the place would very soon become unbearable, like all clubs. But I haven't said that I would use it myself – my own particular imperial territory has long been established. I would confine myself to banking the proceeds after my idea had been put into practice (a far more attractive idea than having your teeth out) and go to live somewhere else. With my new-found wealth I would finance the return to public use of this railway and its poetic route, a practical route too, I'm sure, since it provides a connection for the Auteuil and Versailles lines. Yet the last time I was here, I discovered that the entrance to one of the tunnels had been filled in after all. So there we are, in spite of it all, we must try and place ourselves in the dentist's position, think about the effect of such monstrous tooth decay upon her patients, and not underestimate the huge task accomplished by this lady practitioner. But with its rails now coming to a dead end, the blocked-off railway cutting blots out any inkling of a desire to daydream when one leans on the parapet over the *impasse* of route 29, in the rue Singer. The gardens in this street are always stagnant with the lingering smells of autumn, with glints of its disenchanted ageing light falling on the shoulders of a man in an overcoat whom I've met there several times. Like me, he pretends to be interested in the community clinic amid the questioning and superior glances of the local residents as they come and go with their jingling keys, their unnaturally purposeful step and their poised confidence, while he has nowhere to go in this flagging whirlwind of dead leaves and loves. I keep getting lost in my attempts to get back to the avenue Mozart through short streets sunk in sullen affluence. There is the rare exception tucked away like this working-class hovel still standing in the rue des Bauches beside a family boarding house in which Nerval could have hidden himself away. The avenue Mozart itself, despite its trees, becomes more stand-offish and gloomy as you get nearer to Auteuil. And the same thing happens in the rue Pierre-Guérin, despite the 'hamlets', the bucolic houses scattered about or abruptly grouped together to form a rural fringe. But they seem lifeless, steeped solely in the vanity of upholding their privileged status behind screens of dark shrubs. They share the same concern for keeping up a sleek and intriguing appearance that you can see in

80

the eyes of the young women here, as they slam shut the doors of their cars. Rather than going as far as the church (where, talking of things rural, unless you frame one or two features with great care, there is no balanced pattern of building such as you find in Montmartre or even in Vaugirard) I prefer to go back to La Muette. A dust-haze, straight out of the end of a public holiday, casts its light onto the station roof up towards the park. I am not sure which way to go, then the rue de Passy decides me. This is because in its own way, like certain parts of the rue Raymond-Losserand, or to a lesser extent the rue Saint-Dominique, it expresses a synthesis of every provincial High Street open to pottering about and to shopping and where, in the knowledge that you won't get lost, already registering distances and landmarks from the corner of your eye, you feel you are merging anonymously with the inevitable progress of a human trajectory that never runs in a straight line. So this is what the rue de Passy is like: because of the variety of its shops (though that is disappearing), not present in the rue de Lévis or the rue Cler, which are too taken up with foodstores; and also because its curving line, broken by jutting or receding facades and positioned as it is just beneath the shadow of the Chaillot ridge, places it in the air as the winged centre of an entirely different city, in a completely different climate. And this impression of a place set apart on a height grows stronger when you reach the place Costa Rica, when between two massive corner blocks, half Philip Augustus, half *Prisunic*, the syncopating rue de l'Alboni opens up such a vista that (from the opposite side of a kind of neutral zone occupied by the viaduct) the Bir-Hakeim station marks the first outpost in a scarcely imaginable territory, a Chinese one. So here you are in Kowloon, Macao on a tumble of steps that give onto the square with its varnished plants, Baroque or Victorian architectural detail and the high-fenced platform that looks down onto the roof of the Métro station. I never get tired of looking at the almost silent activity of the blue trains, making the same sound as the wind lightly brushing through birch trees, and even less tired of waiting on the platform itself, which fits perfectly into the hill slope. What am I waiting for? Perhaps one day I shall know but, for the time being, nothing special. I am waiting because it is pleasant to select a holiday resort (one or two hours holiday) in a place which is normally reduced to its function as a mere passing place and somehow obliterated – in the bustle of arrival and departure – by all those distracted people whose brows or jaws are already bent on their own designs; and it is especially pleasant when such a place combines a great many advantages, like this station, acting as it does as a minor but busy customs office, the transition point between the depths of a mountain and the restored space of the sky. The travellers get on, get off (a great many Africans dressed up to the nines, who camp out in the garrets of this district); the trains stop, move off in opposite directions, one towards China and the other towards the Trocadéro. I have my nose in a little book of literary transhumance, written in this part of Paris. It is about counting sheep in a woolly sleep and I hold myself in suspense over it. Then I move off along a vaguely pastoral sentence as meandering as the Lignon river. And now I turn at the bottom of the stairs and, taking the rue des Eaux through the passage which is as steep as a black knife with its blade becoming jagged, through the rue Dickens, where a Sunday afternoon in Edinburgh lurks in a corner, I come to the rue Marcel-Proust where the foundations of the Templars' ksar of the sixteenth *arrondissement* bourgeoisie are embedded, with loophole air-vents for the laundry of the people below, and an arrogant rampart with the highest windows observing the construction of the building on the Left Bank, that urban Florida of further social climbers. The trees on the other bank mark out the gardens of the Turkish Embassy and, beneath the rue Raynouard, the garden of Balzac's house, and both seem to form a single mass of greenery. Yet between the two the rue Berton threads its way. Its name and position give it protection: you just don't really notice it. In it you can find a boundary stone 'placed in 1731 to indicate the boundaries of the seigneuries of Auteuil and Passy' and a kind of totem pole daubed with paint sticking up behind a wall. But you pay no attention to this outlandish feature. You look, without daring to stir, at this street in which the ingenuous heart of the Ile-de-France is buried. You want it to lead nowhere. At the end, like the entrance to a wash-house, is a little blue door.

To the suburbs

Now when as before daybreak the world turns calm and blue again,
I miss the fields and woods which must have been so close
to the spot where the heavy cobbles disappeared into mud and grass.
After it the road rolled on through blue vegetable plots,
beneath all but bare low branches in the blue orchards,
the same clouds like hats slipping by low over the vines,
the same sky moving on in person through the thickets
(I mean a real person whom you know), and then
as in that dream I've had so often and for two years now,
in which I reach one last square on the slopes of Montmartre –
and the city's own dream reveals itself, like this:
dark woods, red horses, hills and golden fields –
you entered the silent depths of the countryside,
Gentilly, Châtillon, Montreuil, Vanves, Clamart and Saint-Cloud.
But north was the really disquieting direction with its strong renewal
    of space,
every plain stretching its thin furrows right up to the seas
and insecurely fastened there along the Oise, along the Aisne and
    Ourcq,
deserted along roads hammered by iron and stars,
swelling and muttering like huge sheets of wrapping paper – the
    north.
These were hard times for people but their innocence was strong.
And they could encounter the Blessed Virgin or the Good Lord
when they looked up from the heavy earth with their illiterate eyes
at the same hour of day as that in which I write:
blue and calm like the depths of a mystic water drop,
and here where I look up to see a mere inch of sky above the concrete
    blocks,
where I lack neither bread, nor warmth nor shirt,
where marvellous means of hygiene and communication are to hand,
reimbursed when I am ill and discontented with my lot,

I try to see this blue sky with the eyes of the poor,
to snatch it, as it moves away so fast, through the holes in a poor
  man's coat.
But it moves away to the north beneath the bridges of the
  Périphérique,
as destitute as those Blacks I saw there near a fire,
the ancient fire of ancient bits of wood and sacks of hope.

With the clouds following the same toboggan slope as the electricity cables, the flat beetfield ripples all over and wings its way between the Vexin and the Valois. But in Hérouville I mistake my route and start to go downhill. When I arrive, I fail to recognize the church that paintings have made so famous. Up above it, divided into bays by white lines, a tarmac platform awaits the tourist coaches. People come to be moved by the graves. I don't go in. I have no taste for such programmed trips to worship places of culture, even though I have a strong belief in the natural divinity of place. But what a sinister and crushing feeling of monotheism there is here, with each tourist standing well-behaved along the nice clean pathway and at the same time, this storage-space chaos of marble, of china and concrete cherubim and (I only take a peep through the porch, but it's typical, the sort of thing you associate with cemeteries, hospitals, waiting-rooms, barracks and museums) that dead weight of boredom and fundamental lack of belief in the hope of a resurrection. There still remains, in various guises, a sort of animistic terror, embodied by the walls, whereas a ritual circle of branches and hymns ought to be sufficient. But apart from being scared stiff, no one gives two hoots for the dead as such unless it be for the saintly lives they led. So let there be nothing mawkish about it. In any case, there is more than enough rewarding abundance in the grass beneath our feet here with the fat bell-tower and the cornfields opposite as they go tumbling down in a great russet-blonde mass beneath the crows, yes, as they do in his paintings of them, but with less hallucination and less stormy blue. Beneath the cornfields, Auvers is merely one long screaming street and the river Oise somehow difficult to locate. Kids on motorbikes skid around in half-turns on the bank that has been widened into an esplanade. Plastercasts have been set out to dry there along with the washing on each storey of the houses. The bikers give me directions. Not very clearly and in a contradictory fashion, but with enthusiasm. The smallest kids particularly, the ones who are only allowed bicycles. Some time later, at the foot of the ramparts that have been cowed into stupor by the tower-blocks at Cergy, I lose my way in the emptying town after leaving that excessively wide bridge, and fate is once again to put me in the hands of some young lads and they will take some pains to look after me. They are honoured, you might say, despite a hint of condescension for my ridiculous cylinder capacity (they go at 125 cubic centimetres), for the idea of being of service excites them and transfigures them a little. As we stop at a red light, the youngest confidently offers me a *Gauloise*, as between equals. But the shyness he has overcome explains his brusque way of doing it and this gift honours me in turn. In fact the streets are deserted, night is falling; this lad has instinctively rediscovered the ancient propitiatory gesture of desert regions when two men who met would entertain the possibility that the other might be a god. Later, these bikers will disappear laconically in front of the station. But for the time being our talk is about gas pipes, and these assume gigantic proportions in the imagination of these lads. I shall hit on these pipes soon enough on my journey: none of them is an obstruction, but that is not true of the trenches that have been dug for them further on and which still await them. They look like old new roads in the clay up towards a factory, and after fifty metres of this, you can't go on. What this stretch of loose rubble will look like in two or three years' time, I don't know: some willow trees perhaps, or possibly a group of depots. No one will enter Pontoise any more as they do now in this almost surreptitious fashion along the river embankments on the left side; I know that from my own experience and from the advice of the fishermen there. Before I go over the fields and follow the short cut they suggest as a possibility, I want to see the river and its huge shapes once more. Its colour comes not only from the equatorial trees that overlook it, but from deep in the water, like the green that is called green for lack of any other colour to describe it. This green rises to darken or to drown with life a being who is both angel and tiger in its huge eyes. I think about forests, springs and Rimbaud. A barge goes by. I listen to the heart-beat of the region in the sound of its engine.

Near to the rue des Bons-Enfants and the rue du Plaisir (where, behind a corrugated iron fence, two cherry trees are starting to fruit), and with a much more pronounced sense of contrast, Saint-Ouen, like Paris itself, has its rue de la Gaîté. The rue des Boute-en-Train leads straight into the flea-market – more exactly known as Malik. Some people seem to think that you come here out of a taste for the decrepit, whereas it is the future that you survey. When electricity, gas and water no longer supply the floors of our homes, and life reverts to living under canvas, right back to ground level, exchange and barter will again become the natural basis of trade. The winds will have sown trees on the balconies of tower-blocks and the chrome taken from vehicles wrecked on the Périphérique will be handed over in exchange for vegetables grown in the holdings of the Railways. Even those districts that are new today will be no more than a fairground, entirely given over to potentially dangerous crowds of people from Belleville to Passy. I can read all this in the as yet unfocused greed on people's faces, during my own obsessional Sunday prowlings about this place. As if I were learning how to ensure my future subsistence, for instance along this alley strewn with boxes and bottles and nails which can certainly be put to reuse. It sucks me along between its two walls, beginning to intimidate me as it grows narrower and narrower beneath a sky that itself grows vaster and vaster, astir with the movements escaping from the clobber laid out on the pavement.

Underneath the concrete bridge, as I expected, I lose my balance all of a sudden and pick myself up again amid shreds of mattresses and tyres. This railway cutting really used to be much cleaner. The local inhabitants, like Dédé the sewage worker, who once showered me with radishes and cherries, were finicky about these things and they used to look after the place. No doubt the Railways, which must still be responsible for it, also looked after it, but since they have definitively abandoned the idea of extending the line to the Eure-et-Loire, they have let brambles run riot and rubbish accumulate all over the place. I move on with difficulty towards a pack of furious mongrels who have scented me from afar and are now pulling at their chain (if with luck there is one) as if they were going to tear the house down, yapping with a dull and muted sound in this dangerous backwater as if they were deep in a wood. The stick I cut in the park to use as a sounding line (since I all but went into the fairly deep canal there) is of little comfort in the face of these dogs jealously guarding their own territory. So I turn back, slashing away at the clinging brambles – I turn back but I hate doing so. From the bridge, what I can see down there, a complex construction amid the flowerbeds, can only be Dédé's Hun palace, made entirely of bits of corrugated iron and sacking. It is true that he had shouted *Come back!* to me, so I wonder why I have let nearly twenty years flee by since then. During this time, blocks of residential flats have overrun the place and created a reaction of hostile, shut-away concealment which I can feel. You cannot go unpunished if you attack the independence of proud market-gardeners-cum-scrap-merchants, experts on the forcing of begonias, and on the patching-up of body work, conscious of man's right to do damn all but sit and smoke for days on end, while the women turn the radio up to full blast and the kids imitate God by dribbling into the dirt to mould it into shapes. I wander about for a long time in search of another way out further on. But it's a wasted effort because everywhere access to the cutting is barred by these sloping banks of laurier-sauce bay trees and concrete, and hereabouts the merest glance would be enough to get you beaten up at the back of the apparently empty residential blocks. I recognize a path that follows along an old wall and which no longer leads anywhere; to the centre of Châtenay-Malabry, to one of the two restaurants saturated in chip-fat and steam. The 195 bus overtakes me and stops twenty-five steps further on; I miss it, preferring to stay on a while and wander about. And here at last is a road that plunges down into a small valley crowned with detached houses and dazed buildings. The valley bed is given over to black-earthed allotments with black sheds that can only be called senile. The faces of the cabbages, blue with strangulation, stare over the fences. I am more or less at ease here, without forgetting the abnormal and almost improbable element of a human presence in a place that is none the less manmade and cultivated, like the Parc de Sceaux earlier with its monumental cascade, its algebraic water surfaces and poplar trees like the ones that persist in these allotments. And I stand here in the mud, embarrassed among the cabbages, with a few shreds of pale sunlight in my hands.

After the splendour, at least this November rust remains and the majesty of its gloom. Among the pools, the laughter of loves that tumbled amid ears of corn and clusters of grapes becomes ultimately unbearable beneath the sun in its decline. At four in the afternoon it is already late daytime in the mud and the dead leaves, as a last robin throbs against the severe pink of the Trianon. You are summoned to this place and at the same time dismissed from it: 'I command it, I have commanded, and every desired command of mine is fulfilled and passes away, in accord with the patience of the wind and the marshes. Commanding – that is all I will have achieved beneath this sky, lying flat itself and overrun with grey beards, facing the slow drawing in of the water, like molten lead, above the steps which are wide but not high enough to raise me above the limits of my realm, a governor still, but conquered by the limitless beyond his power. Thus my posture holds infinity in this flatness, so that I can teach your steps the measures common to bitterness, to splendour and to peace.' (Let's leave a handful of camera-happy Japanese and a few cyclists out of the picture.)

That summer was dazzling, though for me full of menace. I was monstrously lightweight, not a third as old in reality as the still very young person I seemed. So in the morning I used to manage to slip into that box on wheels, the delivery tricycle that left from the rue Liancourt and put me down at Gentilly. At every set of traffic lights we came to, my driver lifted the lid of the box: *Are you all right?* – I was all right. And I would jump out of the box literally like a handsome devil (for I was good-looking and a devil, alas, in those days) in front of a crumbling agglomeration of buildings that were still partly occupied, but not, as one initially supposed, at ground level: quite the opposite, in the upper storeys, where the windows, masking the sun, sported a shapeless code of heaving bedding and washing, while all the other openings had been judged, condemned and summarily executed by means of long black planks and deep nails. People, human wrecks or very old, managed to live in this block of nothing, distressing to see when they leaned out to look down at our goings-on below and my heart, moving along passageways and unsafe staircases spattered with plaster, went out to their imprisonment in a burst of smug, false pity, enjoying the terror of it all. I said I was strange. Once or twice (what I have just called my heart used to repeat this journey), I have furtively gone up the stairs to the last landing, and I knew I was involved in some kind of hideous burglary of this almost peaceful hardship with its stink of soup and latrines, enveloped by a consolatory sky. But, being so young, I was unaware of the fact that there can be no trace of consolation in such places. And then, as usual, once I had gone downstairs, I would visit the concierge to get the big key. There was indeed a concierge who watched over this lamasery of darkness, erected like a big wall around a Christian building that was possibly the remains of a convent in the style of Louis

XIII, now transformed into a depot with its front rising up on the other side from the street, overlooking gardens: lettuces, red-currants, two small children who came and inspected me in silence, lost in the grass and so tiny that I did not dare to say hello to them or offer an orange or a piece of chocolate when I left that enormous low-ceilinged room where I used to take piles of books down from the stacks and went to set out my picnic lunch in the middle of the river Bièvre. Yes, in the middle, using as a table the concrete casing which, like a coffin, confines the putrefied body of sewers in a river that is still fairly unpolluted near to its source, so that a Jesuit naturalist could give it over once more to his brothers the beavers. From here I could see the whole of this priory of mine, set like a bright thought into the dark building against which it stood, with its two rows of windows in a style that always hypnotizes me, tall to the point of seeming too narrow and, despite a film of dust, austerely lucid. Austere, high, cold, dusty, lucid and, in a different way from the surrounding buildings, which were in fact terrible, their window-panes made the fresh June brightness turn pale. What was behind these windows, above my junkroom? Some idle, yet feverish, fumbling about finally made me chance on a door; it took me some time to deal with the padlocked bolt. I entered a tiny room stuffed full of heavy grey sacks hanging there like flying foxes (the cobwebs left by spiders – I only saw one, but one was enough: I swear it was as big as my fist – were stuck there beneath the electricity wires), and to my left I discovered a staircase that led to a pool of light that had been dead since before the beginning of time. More accurately, the negative substance of light, seeming to light the Idea beneath the brows of a metaphysician. In fact all I saw in this storehouse were fat, black-bound treatises on logic or theology, great numbers of them arranged in the right order on shelves that divided the length of the vast room, creating parallel galleries or parallel propositions where – without being able to read anything because of a strong sense of being caught there – in an attempt to understand, I went over, step by step, the terms of an irrefutable argument that was still as closed in on itself as the dim light of the room. No doubt all I had to do was to wait and let myself dissolve into the argument, at which point *something* (if not myself) *would become clear* for certain, and it would have to do with what I had merely skimmed the surface of in the darkness of these buildings, with the radiant blur of the evening over the gardens, in Gentilly on the desecrated, forcibly hidden waters of the Bièvre.

In spite of her baby this young woman has a look which conveys *I wouldn't want to meet the likes of you on a dark night*. I ask her where I can find a station or a 195 bus, and in return I recommend her not to take the path from which I have just come down. She would certainly lose her pushchair up there. Following her extremely precise directions, I find the spot, marked as in Paris by a small post with a red and yellow sign, but the bus does not come. I am writing this on top of a wall, from which I can see the whole plain bolting off towards the woods. It was once fields and now it is turning into a kind of suburban savannah, undulating palely in the bright sunshine. Emus, giraffes even, would scarcely come as a surprise. All that remains of November is the mud from these last days of rain: I've got it to right up above my knees after unexpectedly hurtling down the slope of a big embankment where I was following the path on top, no doubt the transverse wall of a fort with dents for the cannons and traces of good-sized crenellations spiked with tufts of grass. The Bièvre bubbles away below: one of the rare parts of its course not to have been subjected to interference. It seems to gush forth in fury, as if it knew that there was worse to come amid the leek allotments of Gentilly: a voiceless yell inside a concrete casing. But a little higher up on the edges of a building site for a new stadium (run round in circles to your heart's content, but don't stray about), the Buats brook, which probably runs into the Bièvre, lives out the last of its clear, free days unwittingly. In places, dangerous and rather unnecessary planks (it's easy enough to jump across) join the banks where chickens feed and ducks who scarcely disturb the impalpable stream bed and its precious pebbles. A bend in the stream hugs close to the soothing shade of a funerary arbour: beneath a few feet of earth and a tiny monument with horned corners (*From his daughter in loving memory*) lie the bones of the playwright Molé, deceased on the 19 Frimaire of Year XI: *Nature had Showered him with her Gifts, at 68, Death Destroyed All*. Exit Molé; it is already too far in the past for any sadness to be felt. There is a bench. From it you can hear the brook and the birds stitched together, against aggressive background noise from the mechanical diggers, which suddenly ceases. So it must be midday. Mistletoe flourishes in the branches, the bright light drones away in turn like a single soft engine, with accelerations that throw out scarlet tips of branches. *I've been living here since '36* explains the old man whose dog I ran into earlier (one of those black suburban cowering creatures that runs off without acknowledging one's greeting and barks abuse once it's safe behind its fence), and he points to the whole area that has been transformed into walls where corn and lucerne grass once grew, and he doesn't give a damn. I tell him that one day these suburbs will stretch to Marseilles, and this vaguely amuses him. I add that if despite everything I like this devastation and the invasion of disorder (his shed, his allotment, a factory, a brook, two blocks of flats, a folly, a copse, three hundred tyres), it is because I am certain that some apocalypse is in the making here, or at least the promise of one. I notice that deep in his hazy eyes, he doesn't follow a word of what I'm saying. I feel somewhat embarrassed: what apocalypse will there be, what promise, of which I know nothing except that – here, now, on this wall opposite the steppe where I am waiting for the bus that never comes – it will be kept.

Since I have been coming here for years and walked about the surrounding area thirty-six times, I feel it is wrong to situate the Flea Market at the Porte de Vanves because it is really an extension of the rue Didot. Now here I am, wasting far too much time flicking through the old postcards. I am not a collector, but it isn't long before I start adopting the slightly hysterical posture of one, for ever turned to stone except for an invincible flick of the fingertips. A good many of these cards commemorate the 1910 flood: hatted women in boats in the rue de Bourgogne and the rue Bonaparte, and around the crossroads at the end of the rue de Rome, transformed into a pond. But at ten francs a card, you think twice about it. For less than three times that amount I could take away the enamelled metal advertisement for a famous shoe-polish, worded thus in big Cyrillic characters: пион ноар. (But what would I do with it?) The only thing I select is a totally unreal card of the Gare d'Austerlitz, standing there numbed between two masses, one of fog, the other of water: on one side are rows of railway carriages, without wheels, like barges, and on the other, groups of huts that look as if they've turned up straight from the Hudson Bay. In fact, I am less attracted to the picture than to the words, when there are any: *Mummy*, beg Marcel and Claude (from Chaumont-sur-Tharonne in the Loire-et-Cher, dated July 1935), *write to us becoz wee are bord, and for this reason we wood reelly like to cum home*. I take a look at the main street of Chaumont-sur-Tharonne and, for this reason, as these two kids so elegantly put it, I side with Claude and Marcel. Next I sift through piles of pop and rock records which I despise (but a Harold Land is sometimes hidden among them) and, after bargaining, I decide against a set of Quiralu aluminium soldiers out of a helpless feeling about the wrecked childhoods that they represent for me (my own, and that of the brothers in Chaumont whose toys they perhaps were). After this, I find myself in Malakoff. Two metres away from the Boulevard Périphérique, without the least transition, is this utterly different country, as far from having anything to do with Paris as it is from anything in the provinces, even though for me this morning it strangely recalls the Auvergne, but an Auvergne that is not only mythical but also Soviet and Moslem, like Azerbaijan. Perhaps it is because of this clothes market in front of the new town hall. Whereas the old town hall still has a Public-Revenue-Office-cum-Public-Baths-of-Cantal side to it, this new one is all plate-glass and metal, symbolic of the political tendencies – crystal clear, rigid, progressive – of the councillors who put it up. They are no doubt also responsible – at the other end of the Sentier du Tir where a real gas-lamp hiccoughs like a pilot light – for commissioning the copious fresco in pre-Colombian–Marxist and Auvergnat style, inscribed with two lines from Neruda. Behind it, a twenty-three storey block of flats shoots up like a cannon blast without disturbing the character-istic local gloom of the brick suburban houses and the spindle trees. No discordance is apparent. On the contrary, it seems (deceptively as it happens) as if every street were exactly the same and that this is why, for ambiguous reasons either of philanthropy or of orderliness, the street signs carry not only their own names, but also those of the street from which you have come and the one you will arrive at, indicated by arrows. Yet the deceitful lie of the land here has an undermining effect that causes you to skid; the irrational, in cosy guise, lies in wait for you at every corner, and you lose your way either in the direction of Montrouge or towards Vanves, amid these parcels of the infinite where everything holds tightly together yet loses hold at the same time, like the groups of nomads who have come down from their mountain for the lottery, like the hair of the young women I meet and run into again, amid piles of blue denim jeans and displays of fruit, with such indecision written in their sequinned, wasp-like eyes.

The transcendental North of the Scottish poet exists, I am convinced of it. But I am infinitely grateful that, to attain it, it is not necessary to immerse oneself in spiritual exercises. To tell the truth, it might just be possible, at the Porte Pouchet, to get there by train, for despite the sorry state of the tracks down here in this cutting, a branch line of the Ceinture railway goes there. You can sense the roundness of the city behind you like a compass, and beyond the lowering presence of an off-putting piece of construction – a kind of huge storage plant that generates counter-energy – you can see the track that had floated along in buckles up to this point, jetting out into a fan and obeying the laws of magnetic attraction. The rails then sink like arrows into the polar region of rusty blue fog. A sudden shiver reminds me that I must follow them without delay, and I don't mean a vague twitch of the soul or the intellect but genuine goose-flesh, the very breath of the North right there on my skin. But first I need to find a way of getting down there (you always manage to find one; there is always an iron rung missing or, between the ground and the fence, a hole made by cats through which you can sometimes squeeze, surprisingly enough); next, you must take no notice of an emerging human shape a bit further along; it freezes for a second and then contorts itself wildly before it disappears beneath the brambles on the embankment. This character had thought, like you, that he was the only person there, or more precisely the last, and with nothing to indicate your transcendental purpose to him, your strange attitude of caution was enough to give him a good fright into the bargain. None the less, after two-hundred bold steps, I go back up, beneath the inscrutable gaze of a cats' tribunal. For I am thinking of the many times I have had the same experience, walking like this towards the absolute, and becoming, like the rails, a needle with a finer and finer point which becomes magnetic and ends up returning to the bosom of the ideal mass, shining brightly. And I returned to my senses slumped on the grass in a street of factories, in the middle of the very real nullity of Gennevilliers or Saint-Denis. And now I am flushed with shame and relief, like a predestined person who is losing his nerve. But after passing by the island covered in a squared patchwork of allotments and flanked with rows of barges as cavernous as the tombs of kings; after moving about in the combat zone around the basilica; after crossing bridges where the beat of a bull's pulse can be sensed halfway across; after going through huge depots of petrol or uranium to the accompaniment of warning whistles – I now none the less come back to my senses and discover where I am, and nothing has stirred. The place is dominated by the calm that succeeds the worst cataclysms, even after they have been forgotten, and the sky, prehistoric again, grazes with an innocent lack of haste on the ultimately ecstatic extent of the damage. That part of being which goes back beyond time looks at the world through the eyes in my head, and my legs transport it automatically onto an embankment. There I search in vain for the sun in this pulverised light, which is slightly more dense where the rails come to an end and flatten out towards the north.

Will they eventually knock down this fringe of hovels embedded along the city ring-road, the sign that it is going straight
back into sick infinity, with the surrounding hills beneath a
strong, Technicolor sky, delighted with the roar of sixteen-
wheeler tankers making for the main junction? Yet the blue of
the sky still belongs to a former age, beneath this clump of trees
where, despite the noise, I might be reading a slim, calf-bound
volume full of passionate remarks about the equality of men and
Nature. Behind the abattoirs the plaster minarets of the Sacré-
Cœur rise up in the background of a landscape stricken with
violet light. I am not speaking of happiness or misfortune. This
light strikes down like a declaration of something. A declaration
of love, an announcement of death, but kindling emotions that
are shining in the frightened grass, the metal and the concrete.
And the shabbier houses are present at the scene like a crowd,
rows of people crushing against each other and hoisting
themselves upon each other's shoulders around some enormous
accident, striking up a chant of horror or celebration. I don't
know Pantin very well. There must be an old people's home
functioning between its two cemeteries because the quiet and
immaculate streets are lined with benches on which groups of
three or four old ladies no longer even attempt to gossip as they
await the evening and perhaps remember, or don't remember.
The rue des Pommiers cuts across the long rue de Candale,
which goes on staircasing up as far as the district borough of Les
Lilas. The rue de Bel-Air follows the lower part of this rise, and,
taking the rue de Bellevue or the rue des Panoramas, you
continue up a steep slope until you come to a kind of belvedere
at the end of the rue du Garde-Chasse that overlooks the chalk-
dust expanse to the north. A tramp is eating, bending with his
elbows on the ground; a group of young people are chatting in
front of a big motorbike. I go down again through the rue

Marcelle. Between nos. 46 and 52 there are two numbers missing because an overgrown orchard breaks the row of detached houses built in different styles. Half submerged by the yellow and blue grass on a tumbling slope, pear trees create a figure from ancient science against the horizon. The orchard itself embodies the diagram of a memory as transparent and lost as that of the ladies of Pantin. I interpret and decipher as best I can this esoteric design of posts, branches and stones. But the dominant impression is of the voice inside me repeating *you see* and nothing more than that: *you see,* in the same persuasive tone as this sad, soft orchard.

The Benediction of Saint-Serge
for Nicole

So much charcoal beneath the priest's eyes can only kindle a flame.
When he moves down from the pavement you will see it shine,
dense as the sensuous oil of mortification
(and soot has left its trace on Veronica's veil
her face more nocturnal and more softened towards sin).
At the back of the alley the black trees stretch out against a mauve
*   sky.*
Over the church front of fretted household wood
climb the sloping Slavonic characters gaunt and pointed,
and the church inside is also like the blackened base of a lamp
swaying in the wind with our two hands joined over Paris.
I find it hard to grasp the symbolic ritual of this scene,
as the bearded officiant looms up from an isba at the side,
in one hand his book, in the other the tiniest candle.
Then he returns and the voices resume a droning psalmody of
roaming lark song and roundels of love on plains.
Meanwhile the forests hug the city in their soft embrace,
as they did when Princess Anna in her dungeon saw
the snow bound Ukraine venture boldly to the banks of the Seine,
with their lynx-like breaches in the sky on the watch for your eyes.
She has crossed the Opéra, the insurance-company blocks,
heard the clucking teal in the hollows of the Marais,
climbed the slopes to les Batignolles or to Pigalle
and the stations where rails flee off like quivers of spears.
But were you already on your way down from Belleville to meet me,
a silence in the future rumble of trains and building yards?
The cantors fall silent and are blowing now on candles. Listen to
all these words, these footsteps, suspended henceforth in the night;
the wind blows up your hair over the centuries and the ruins
with the star that rises in the murky water of the Ourcq canal.

II

Walking Bass

When you leave Paris from the Gare d'Austerlitz, the very first thing you see are these depots built like luxury hotels in Cannes. The railway system spreads out again and brings the same sense of contentment. Where the lines start branching out, the cuttings are hemmed in by embankments on which weeds and sly bushes make their protest. They must be hard to reach and what is more, they are forbidden territory, but a darkly-disguised man sometimes manages to stretch himself out on them, dreaming with his eyes open, while the cast iron goes on striking endlessly against the steel of suspension springs. Hundreds more railway coaches of all kinds, but motionless ones, stand there expecting nothing to happen any more. And as we move off along volleys of widening rails that envelop narrow lives with no apparent centre or misery about them seen from their gardens, railway coaches appear, seeming forever forgotten, already almost absorbed by this small community of bricks and lilac where isolated tracks provide their moss-yellowed sleepers for fencing. And then some day or other, decisions are made that cause even these coaches to stir. They jolt towards the points, and our man on the embankment hears them, distinguishing very acutely between the hollow echoing of the tank-wagons and the dull echo inside the old wooden coaches. But all this traffic goes on distantly above his head, which is aimlessly exposed to the sky and its indifferent blue, grey, or black.

Right in the middle of nowhere, these railway depots are still standing with almost every window missing. If you look through, you can see the sky dragging along the railway tracks. A very small goods truck is coming down a slope on its own, brick-red. Closer by there are more of them gleaming with fresh spinach-green paint. And in the background there are still more, whole convoys of them, padlocked, sullen and motionless. Just beyond these shunting yards there are gardens scattered about the place, strewn with evidence of human emotion: tools, toys, washing, rabbit hutches. Then, without any transition, comes a copse of birch trees in a marquetry pattern of mother-of-pearl and ash-tinted rice paper. But before this we had crossed the fortification zone: ochre couch-grass, low flights of steps, and the blurred contours of the outworks, just like an excavation site. As places of entrenchment and bombardment their significance is gone. The rounded levees of grass and porous rock above the half-filled ditches create a geomancy for the abandoned worship of a god. Then, between one tunnel and the next, through the spurs beneath which it winds its course, you constantly rediscover the Marne, tilting as it bends without losing a single drop of its water. For it is the train that is tilting as it starts to cross bridges, and this water is merely following its own separate gliding power. There is power in the whole landscape too. Rather low and devoid of gracefulness, but very compact and strong, like the squat belltowers halfway up slopes beneath patches of yellow earth and copses. The crumbling edges expose the chalk beneath the surface, which rolls down towards the spangled rubbish among tin cans and tyres. The same dull white between chinks in the clouds, the sun pours out a brightness onto the countryside, worthy of its solid resignation. In fact nothing raises itself up with any sign of protest or with too many expectations, apart from the occasional copse, in the briefest of explosions. Right in the middle of the bends in the river there are excavations in the sand that no longer serve any purpose and stand there reflecting. Here again, the residual traces of an excavating project are remodelling themselves into small wooded islands and crumbling river-banks, in the same way as the outcrops, the forts, the hills and even the shapes of the flight of the rooks over the steely surface of the flood water. And thus the world in its deafness is obstinately jubilant. Piercing through the increasingly rare gaps in the greyness, the beams of the sun raise a pollen that is scarcely less milky than the Marne, which from now on is at the same level as the plain, covered with fields and salvoes of branches as they throw out their mistletoe. The factory, with a dense crowd of workers emerging, is doing the same thing, and the train fleeing across the scene shares in the will to achieve the same end.

When they are wet, the rich stretches of brown earth on the slopes can even turn purple with excitement. A path goes off below and carries me away. I know them, the stories to which this path and its grass plume lead; I sense them or I remember them. They all have to do with the moment when someone goes off among the woods into this tumult of blues that are as pale as his anger. And once more I cross over the Marne, exasperated by a downpour of rain, with the sky black all of a sudden, and other paths turning off beneath further cargoes of scudding clouds, weighing so heavily everywhere you look that a molten oven cracks open and spills low over the hills. The rest of the story is insignificant: gestures and words that crumble. Now, on my way again, I am interested only in these silent beginnings and endings before the hurtling night – and once more the sky is moved to fury and gentleness; then comes the end, when all I have to do now is to place my head against the train window, amid those rare lights dotted in the spiteful reflection of my eye.

An increasingly dense blackness announces the end of the night. It explodes back over suburban stations in the full throes of walking in their sleep. The people stationed beneath the lamps (and there are never enough lamps) have a shadowy existence. It is not clear what is going on in their minds, still heavy with the heat, with premonitory hopes and dreams they had not asked to have. But for some of them a kind of ecstasy persists: they lean forward without the least attempt to stir. From one disconcerted platform to the next which explodes like a mine, something that can no longer be called space imposes the likelihood of a world without history and without the play of movement. Merely an amorphous substance that weighs down and swells in great clumps. Then the rolling of enormous dice cast in the interval redistributes a logical chaos of houses. You can only distinguish the lighted windows that constantly move about in orthogonal leaps, using the same exact and indecipherable notation as the stars. Making a funnel with my hands, I blot out all the reflections of the compartment in the depths of the carriage window; I am on the lookout for a premonitory sign of daylight in the passing glimpses I get of the countryside. And there it is, fleeing already in the bend of a stream or of a pale path pitted with puddles, while the ink-drenched sky presses down like a blotting-pad, submerging the hills, the undergrowth where animals, awakened by the noise of the train, are surely breaking through the dead thickets. Quite high up towards the east there comes a collapse in the clouds and two or three streaks of Prussian blue. And here is the first light of day expanding once again, that initial thrust from the hissing turbine of the sun. Then the light stabilizes itself in a hollow in the greyness into which the whole day will slip, and it will be good. A long day on the rails, a day of telegraph poles and iron bridges flooding past against the hillsides, their rounded slopes darting with pointed churches. Like someone tightly tucking back their knees in order to get back to sleep at all costs, the small towns show resistance amid a jumbled wreckage of wooden planks and cranes, piles of car bodies and gardens with individualistic potting sheds, underpants on the line, small fires that have been choking in their own smoke since the day before. But quietly amid this disarray a pattern of secret lives will rally. Near the signal-box and the footbridge, there is always one of those boulevards that rise up along the track, quite aimlessly. And, often, since it is still early, or else too late, or because of its thankless position away from crossroads, this boulevard is inhabited solely by concrete, privet hedges and neon café signs on the corners of blocks of flats made of old cardboard. And sometimes a young woman will be walking up this boulevard with a suitcase that seems too heavy. She stops for a second and, without seeing it (simply because she is standing there and it has just passed by under her nose), bent a little on her hip, utterly unconscious of her beauty, forgetful of the overcast day that is floating by like her fate, she watches the train as it disappears.

The Yonne provides for itself so well between its banks that it seems to bulge up in the middle. The entire countryside is stuffed full. It is cold, then it is hot, beneath the breaks and the effusions of the asphalt clouds released by the south wind. A few kilometres after Sens, hills start jumping up on the right bank, with dark clumps of trees that foreshadow the forests and gorges of the Côte-d'Or. But suddenly, and while we are moving along beside one of those canals with old stone edging, in the style of Louis XIII and yet Chinese, a heavy metal impact is felt beneath the compartment. The train soon draws to a halt. Two-hundred faces make a sudden appearance, amused but already on the point of showing anxiety. Guards get down to patch up a metal plate as best they can. We move on and then stop again. A telephone message is sent from Saint-Florentin-Vergigny to inform Dijon of the problem. Meanwhile, the ethereal young girl who has been walking the whole length of the packed train since Laroche comes in and asks me if this seat is free (*Yes, indeed*, I reply) and without taking any further notice of me or of the rather ropey axle that is supporting the carriage, she goes straight to the window seat and becomes enveloped in a blue nimbus.

Nothing but an algebraic tangle of rails and catenaries for comfort. For why do I have to leave? I am going off without the least enthusiasm in the direction of that gloom-inducing mountain and its oppressive weight. Just now, in the boulevard Saint-Marcel, in a shop window, I saw that *Jesus the Tailor makes to measure*. Further along from this, a small and utterly ordinary street goes down to join a small nondescript square that was shaking itself among its leaves like a girl in a bath. That is all I saw. But the city displayed its soul as completely at a loss, again like a girl who won't make the decision for herself, who turns, seems to reflect, and waits without it being possible for you to interpret her gaze or her gestures; but if you approach her she is at once intrepid and humble (and above all wordless), aware of her own depths like the water in a dam on the verge of collapse. And so her eyes opened at the end of every avenue, now grey, now blue, always with the softness of something that does not focus properly but dreams, dreaming me up too as I waver between *oblivion* and *perhaps*, a passer-by. I don't know what I am glorifying in the depths of this impassive stretch of space: my own calculated indifference or else the clement remoteness of a god. One thing is certain: I said *leave me alone* and that is a harsh enough thing to say. Yet I did not choose the words. Otherwise I would have tried to live up to them, even in this commentary that takes my abuses to the limit. (It is desirable that I should express myself here in a more modest and clearer fashion, but I am not yet utterly mad.) Let us proceed: he who is tormented by a sometimes crazy need for solitude exposes himself, among other disadvantages, to the awareness of alarming increases in the degree of his private criminality. And indeed, I am in the process of executing the awful, unstoppable junior executive who has assumed the right to tyrannize the railway compartment like a departmental boss, his nickel-plated eye gunning me down as he turns the pages of a vaguely left-wing weekly which he is energetically gutting, *flick! flick!* as if he were going through job advertisements. From then on I consider myself to be acting in self-defence – but God forgive us, him you, me, as we travel along in this shaking box through the Montereau / Laroche-Migennes section of our destinies. Jesus makes our clothes to measure. I think again about God and Satan. I should prefer to be sitting above the rue des Pyrénées at the point where stairs rise up over a hellish arch, as far as the bridge that strategically joins the cemeteries of Charonne and Père-Lachaise. The last time I was there, as in a tear-jerking tale, I saw a lad climb up these steps with his stick of bread, and rush by (though not too fast) when he got to this dreadful chasm – the smell of piss, iron girders, a cabal of rubble beneath the sooty grime, the dark underside of love. I was sitting up above near my moped – don't you dare come near me! – like a fallen Lucifer. I think more and more that his sin was not so much pride as fatigue, boredom, even a kind of humility that incited him to seek out places overrun with nettles, bits of pavement, frozen in the posture of a sorry specimen of a man, disturbing and yet dangerous, I know that well enough. Meanwhile we have crossed the opulent countryside of the Yonne and here are the green hills of the Auxois. Vercingetorix is busy coughing in the clouds that have just broken up like old-time steam on the track. For the six-hundredth time in this incomprehensible life, I am going to get my connection in Dijon.

Not far from Besançon the line runs along beside huge piles of scrap metal, right next to a reprocessing plant. And there stands the diminutive old locomotive, on its very best behaviour, one of those models that had become fit only for depot work. Now it is awaiting its turn to be shoved into the grinder, if it can be said that a locomotive, even an old one, can be waiting for anything at all. And are we going to start crying our eyes out over a construction of pistons, wheels and a boiler? No, I don't think so. But hang on a minute, this one that is pulling the carriage of your own period of waiting, you poor old steam-driven bodies, you poor human feelings destined for the scrap heap, and who then will reprocess you? There will always be some weakling beyond hope of recovery, dragging his soul and his feet in the rubble, picking up the shattered rubbish of whatever kind of life he can find: and what then? Nothing, is the answer, since everything moves on frantically, heave-ho! there go the trains, the tanks, the cost of living index, the political speeches, the prose of academics, onward march! for the grand brotherhood of slaughterers with their bombs and their show trials, and already the jaws of those in the know are moving up and down like power-hammers; and God's sweet sunlight gleams on the old machine's brass fittings.

Mills with an important industrial potential have preserved their appearance of basilicas or fortified castles. But the further you move into Champagne the more pointed certain steeples become. In this region which I have travelled through and observed so many times, I ought to be seeing nothing at all any more. Now, on the contrary, as time goes by, I become increasingly wide-eyed (I've taken a book with me but only for when it gets dark), and with my forehead pressed against the carriage window, which is vibrating and teaching me something about speed, as long as daylight cares to last, as long as the amazement with which the daylight has been struck increases and forces space to contain the extent of its own decline – for the hills are receding and underground shapes unfolding because long fingers are searching for something feverishly as if beneath a sheet – my gaze is passionately fixed on these easily recognized signs that have not changed but remain as fresh as the ones I am discovering simultaneously, like this small hump-back bridge with neither road nor stream. In fact there is nothing that is not a reason for surprise, or rather for stupefaction. Perhaps if I were to manage to describe every single thing, at the very moment when the least blade of grass or bit of wire appears, I should understand what mobile part I play in this rhythm, in this order ecstatically governed by a strong hand everywhere – from the movements of five lads kicking a football to this black mistletoe set out in the poplar trees like a musical score. Particularly this evening when every detail stands out with an inevitability, yet with a freedom from constraint in that same fated inevitability. So many centres around which the whole world is organized and from which it spreads in calm whirlwinds of evenly balanced points: sheds, woods, ponds, slopes, the pink fulminating cotton blown from the furnaces at Thionville, or those piles of logs divinely stacked up at the end

117

of a platform. But I am a mere point, one that disappears at the intersection of two curves, shaped into a pointed arch by the rails and the setting sun.

After ten minutes' halt in front of this thicket of points, we finally move off again without the least jolt, like a sigh. Things start fumbling about in the indistinct darkness: headlights, green lights, some of them cyclamen-coloured, a shade more glowing than the precursory halo of the sun, frozen to the east. Barrels of tar emerge from the heavy tatters of dancing torchlight, rounding up the eyes of the night from the depths of the shunting-yards – all around, in the sky seen through the crossed, round-riveted bars of iron bridges. But gradually the sorting-out of the darkness proceeds: a wall, a shovel, visible again in the dark muddle facing the light as it spreads with inflexible softness up to the moment when you think it might waver, with six birch trees lending the only supernatural note to the scene, the ruins of a factory becoming visionary even before the sun starts swaying like a little orange boat in the reeds.

On the horizon the ghostly white building like a church must be a silo. Ever since this morning the air has been gently dusty as on threshing days, and for almost an hour you could have said: evening is coming on. Château-Thierry, Epernay go by. Well before Bar-le-Duc, it is night would be the only appropriate way of describing this deep blue ice that has settled on the scene before breaking into stars over the hillsides. The nearest woods are now stricken with holy terror, gripped by belligerence. In the meantime, mists of pink gold have risen from the stubble-fields and the maize, bringing back the nectar of colour in the same way that you feel the summer heat evaporating out of stones. A small group of tiled rooftops and, immediately after, the walls of a brickworks put the finishing touches to love. Not the blind fornication that pumps away towards orgasm, but the incandescent suspense in which two bodies levitate together for a second and for ever. Love has no name, no limit: it infuses itself. While I was writing and pretending to do vague equations on the left-hand page so as not to draw the attention of two engineers, darkness installed itself and with no trace of a star. If the lights on the train were to go out, you would certainly be able to see, from far off in the countryside around, love gleaming through me.

The rails run close to the furrows in this well-ploughed field and they, in turn, musically follow the bends in the Marne. In spite of many signs since departure (those empty trains moving around in shunting-yards, the tall signal-boxes with their clicking brains) it is the curve of this ploughed field that leads me back towards the inspired character of man. For instance, man is mad and really frighteningly so. Today's fresh newspapers on the platform inform us that people are killing all over the place and potential murderers prowl about, worse still, murder whimpers away in so many hearts. Then here is a singing field, a fat woman hanging out the washing in a garden, long, crumbling old walls around a farm with chickens, a grey horse amid copses that have had to be planted. And I think back to another sign, almost nothing, a mere row of stakes rhythmically hoisting themselves up on a hillside – so there we are. Over all this is the early-morning mist of light, its soft, unbending hosanna. For skulls are heavy, legs are heavy, and whole bodies become so heavy that they need to be quickly buried. Heavy bells then start to toll in villages and I do not hear them. But they were ringing through the drone of a plane which woke me up earlier, just before daylight, among the small gardens of Asnières, lying beside my double who was moving away from the density of September in her dream: woman and leaves, distant worlds. The powerful tenor voice of a motorcyclist passed by outside. I recognized the *Song of the Partisans* drowning the noise of his engine. And in the bed that is now spilling over with the swift dawn, we linger before the darkness in our eyes and the bitter-tasting crannies of our mouths. So much so that we had to hurry to leave, forgetting to feed those mad cats and to bring the rose, picked when the moon had risen askew with the 'flu. Next the bridge, the Périphérique, Ornano, Barbès, Magenta. Luckily the people at the Gare de l'Est had mislaid the shunting engine, so there was a respite during which we managed to avoid cursing and complaining (*write to me, you're leaving, you will come back*). But I still managed to bang my head – bong! bong! – against the metal side of the carriage, with three or four drops from my old lemon of a soul between my eyelids and once more the teeth of those carnivorous little goldfish in my leg; they will get bigger and time, too, tears us apart – that's good – otherwise what would we know of love, we plastic hearts? And once again we have picked up a good speed – that's good – the points succeed each other like the verbs in a precise sentence, and soon we shall come to the field that has reminded me of the inspired nature of man and the mystery of his plight.

Stops, station buffets, road links

Once again I am going to start crying in the corner of this station buffet. At least the people on the opposite platform will be able to content themselves with the thought that I am just sneezing. I am all alone here. And I cry my eyes out in this solitude as if I were still about to meet up with someone I haven't seen for months. It was on a different evening, in October. Impossible to stop me crying, but it won't last. I wonder what does last. I asked myself the same question during all those hours on the rail-car in the black Jura, during the train connections made in the rain and the waits at halts with those cross-barred clocks. and here I am again with the staggering answer to my question: there are no words for it; merely this shadowy void of a station buffet, my head against the window so that, from a distance, people will imagine that I am coughing or being sick. Maybe. It has rained without a break, except for that day I went through the vineyards towards the lake, between the hardened cities of bank and casino. I think that the house, back there on the grass road, had been dead for a long time beneath the ill-fated mountain, and that ultimately love has no power. So even when it is felt most intensely it needs to shout, as I am crying now (and how she did shout with that over-powering, terrifying voice of hers, back there in the house). So who holds this power? I must have some inkling since here I am, at my age, still crying – but I don't want to know. Instead I allow myself to be totally cut into pieces by these claws, piece by piece until the bitter end, but always under protest. So I start crying in this buffet. I order a glass of red wine, another, a third, then I leave. From the square you can see the hills, the fat clouds placed there upon the light that is as dense as water. I sit in the sun to have a smoke. Switzerland must be the only place you can get this wonderful Maryland tobacco. Leaning back on my bag, I sniff the air, and with a towel bearing the Bundesbahn motto, I dry my sweet eyes.

The fair starts just after the wing of the building bearing the sign *Public Baths*: it threads along the quayside, the shooting-galleries on the right with rifles and bunches of feathers, and on the left a few roundabouts, and not a cry coming from them. Arabs in their Sunday best stand apart, meditating, and on the benches between the booths retired couples doze off. The fairground people themselves stand with their backs to the deserted esplanade. In an aluminium fog over the newly-built factories on the outskirts, in the gardens where people stand looking at the smoke from heaps of grass that were scythed the day before, the daylight goes on and on fading. There is so much space around the place that it is better to stand still, or to go round in circles like the wooden horses with no music.

for Marceau

Several of the villages here have their names suffixed with the words *en-montagne*, in spite of the fact that there *is* no proper mountain, merely more or less powerful waves that overlap each other and unfold towards the Saône, the Loire, and the last folds of the Côte-d'Or and the first folds of the Morvan. So you go down, you go up, and what you mainly notice is something freer in the air that doesn't come from the escarpments or these two pronounced hilltops – Chamilly and Les Trois-Croix – but from the way the landscape opens up, after a succession of terraces, onto the valley below without any steep drop, and beyond, three times in a century perhaps, onto the spectre of Mont-Blanc. Many houses in the surrounding area are going to ruin. But barns that are still kept locked and five or six chickens are signs that people live here. There used to be wooden-bead curtains dancing in front of doorways: the same sort of curtains in yellow and green plastic stir a little further on at the top of solid stairways above wine cellars one or two steps deep. With the church, the town hall and the café so far apart, the raised square at the centre of the village seems unnecessary and deserted. But when an old man with a flannel belt comes and walks across it you can still see signs, in the midst of this neglect, of a slightly negligent but tranquil existence coming to life – pots of flowers and newly-painted shutters, a scrap of aggressive asphalt or of wrought-iron luxury, even a few children. As evening comes on, they start to pick quarrels with each other in the dust, and their cries can be heard. The voices resonate completely differently from the way they do in the valley: they rise up, seem to shine and then suddenly cease; nothing stops them carrying or smothers them. These voices are a better indication than a mountain peak of the sense of the words *en-montagne*, together with the gaze of this old man, not used to passing visitors, the rest of his life being merely barren *teuppe* (to

125

use his dialect) or work on the vineyard slopes. Yet the mystical centre of the region is a real mountain block from which terraced slopes spread themselves out to the north towards the rock faces of Le Bout-du-Monde, and to the west an area of mines that quickly came to nothing. All that is left of this now is a row of grim-faced houses built for the workforce, administrative buildings that look like redoubts or toll-houses, and here and there the tracks of a railway cutting through roads and meadows. The best of the landscape is towards the south, the point of the crescent that unfolds for thousands of acres from Santenay to Nuits-Saint-Georges. So the best thing you can do is to sit in the café and ask for white wine. Red would be less suitable for the time of day and its over-brimming brightness, for this slightly harsh mountain atmosphere. The bar is made of dark wood and behind it there is an ancient glass-fronted case for cigarettes. The café inside is right next to a kitchen, half of which is used for storing sacks of fertilizer and drums of sulphate. and here a neighbour who has not come in to drink is stationed, uttering unhurried statements of the obvious in the local sing-song tone of resignation, his back to the daylight that is as completely unharnessed as his syllables.

Far away down there, small trawlers are coming up the estuary at high speed: red, blue, green. This bridge is strange, spanning not so much the sky as the years of my life, the years when we used to take the ferry to Brouage and stay here for hours staring at the mud and the boats grounded in it at the edge of the dazzling surface of water. Today you move straight across an era that is fast disappearing, like these coasts of black wooden hulls that look like rotted sperm-whales. I am not sure I miss it. And it is very beautiful, seen from up here in the air. Yet this bridge inevitably takes something away from the scene, at least the moment when we used to float, sheltered beneath the horizons in a spherical overspill of light. A kind of indecision remains in spite of everything, the swirl that comes and stirs up the space at the centre of an immense pearl, where the flattest part of the land goes to merge with the ocean you can never see. The delight of merging with things: up here, you look down on the scene with ease, as from a plane. Yet I prefer to stick to the pavement, because I have no head for heights. That is, I don't feel sick, but I am grabbed by an almost irresistible urge to plunge down, and I know what I am capable of. I am thinking about the thoughts I would have on the way down. I am standing exactly above a tiny boat in which five fishermen are crammed together, as if they were petrified in tar. This sodding bridge is now starting to dance, so I cling tight to the guardrail.

There are surely (even in Brest, sighted from afar beneath mist) specialists capable of undoing the feelings I get in relation to anything that looks like a redoubt, a fort, even a small one, an oven, an entrenchment, a blockhouse, a depot and the various debris of the army or industry, but I don't really care. I too could use my vagrant impulses to achieve the same end, but I don't really want to do so. So I suddenly start off along paths marked by a yellow signboard with black stencilled letters, a bit skew-whiff – DANGER MILITARY ZONE NO ENTRY – because I couldn't give a damn about such signboards either. No doubt the thing that awaits me at the end of the path is always close to disappointment, but such disappointment cheers me, simplifies my existence and transforms me almost religiously into a pure expectation of nothing. In fact all these buildings serve no purpose any more and this is what stirs me. Some of them have dates inscribed on the front (1883, 1813) and, in order eventually to merge into it in a few centuries' time, they are already sinking into the indistinct density of the ground. Other buildings seem to be temples, hopping-mad from top to toe, and bitter gods, stagnant like the weeds in ditches, have filled the space once allotted to heavy-bored weaponry. Tramp gods, expelled from real places of worship, with no faith or hope in themselves left, they wallow on heaps of plastic cartridges and rubble. Who honours them? Unwittingly, obsessed passers-by who scratch their initials or dreadful graffiti into the plaster, and now my own immobility and my silence. They give out no sigh, no reply, but I don't demand any: I can feel they are really there, much nearer and possibly more dangerous than in the middle of the row of menhirs where I took up position this morning, contemplating the ruins of the Poet's country mansion on the horizon: it looked like what had been a small lime works.

I brake so suddenly that my back wheel skids on the verge, in sand and gravel. It's my bag throwing me off balance. Never mind, I shall lose another ten minutes while the storm gets worse and I am not even halfway there, still following alongside a railway on my right, somewhat drab but cared for: there is no trace of grass on the rusty pebble track and although they have no gates, which are really no use for path crossings, the crossing points are signposted. What has come over me? At the very point where the line starts bending away sharply from the road, for nearly twenty metres the left-hand rail and the sleepers have disappeared. This means that here, and for how long now? no train passes any more, but the bend is still there and goes on plunging down behind a bridge, towards who knows what region of stranded carriages turning to rust. Of course I hear nothing, of course nothing has happened and nothing will happen apart from this insistent absence, as if the twenty metres of torn-up rail did not stop me going on, not that, but threw the pattern of time out of order, panting in the impartial silence that heralds impending catastrophe.

The irresistible sun climbs in the chestnut tree on the terrace.
A rusty bell and another silver one pick out the quarters of the hour.
I wait for a third in gold which would mean: time has stopped –
time but not the sequence of my liberated movements.
For in a second I shall go and collect my heavy backpack and resume
this morning's lighter walk from fountain after fountain to the Lime
    Tree.
Yet I seem to have been punched by a dizzying fatigue,
my head and the sky bursting with a thousand black dots
turning to the scattered whirlwind of birds over the Sarine
against the rock where Fribourg raises its Tibetan brow.
I doubtless slept too little in that curious inn
where my arrival at first raised such stupor.
As if it were not normal to ask for a room
in a place already marked by a board reading ZIMMER FREI,
the regulars in the bar eyed me with embarrassment
(but clearly less for themselves than for me)
and the lady near the counter fled to another,
the other to a third, each more jumpy than ants
hastily transmitting a message through quivering antennae,
until return to calm with the old lady in black,
squat and severe, offering merely a fairly dignified distrust,
with the key to room 18 in one hand, my sixteen francs in the other.
I imagine that today the sweet quartets of little girls
on May Day will not shun the doors of this house.
Their song is rather out of tune for the reputation of this town
and I ask myself – and them – what they will do with the money.
We share it, *one tells me and a second adds,* It's for Mother's Day.
And now I'm walking up the main street full of fruit and flowers.
There are no cards of Chez Simone *for sale –*
and I withhold my reasons for wanting such a memento,
for fear it will end in the inauguration of a plaque

and speeches. The sun climbs and soon it will jump
the slender hurdle of midday which trembles as it goes,
as I tremble on my quick return across the Zaehringen bridge.

The little station, so tranquil as daylight fades beneath the hills, is protected by the forest, and loved by the sun, now almost as low as the church steeple, in the way that, at this time of day, the sun loves and ripens everything. It was once a stopping-place of some importance, and this is attested by several engine sheds and numerous loop-lines and sidings between the platforms, where all that lingers on in the gently unkempt grass is the wind from the Vosges and from time to time a traveller, brought there a little too early for the evening train. At first he stands there uncertainly, for a long time, shouldered by the unflinching sunlight. But neglecting his suitcase – probably a light one – and the No Admittance signs, he crosses the tracks as far as the high, abandoned mound, follows by it, passes a depot, a goods train and finally the black suspended bracket on which the green lights shine out steadily. There is nothing else beyond this, over towards a dark blaze of branches, except railway tracks gathering together and stretching out into the distance like a whiplash. This is undoubtedly where the train will appear, exactly on time, and it would be strange to discover that it never came. Yet so much tranquillity and silence have gone to sleep on time here that it is even stranger to see the train appear.

for Georges Perros

I have been circling beneath the mountain for nearly a good two hours and the rain persists. A fine rain, cold, disciplined. It is not going to stop. I have nevertheless vowed, to the spirits or the gods of this mountain, that I will go up and sacrifice to them the little that I am carrying in my saddlebags (biscuits and chocolate) if they grant me a beam of sunlight, even a very pale one, for the climb, or at any rate the momentary suspension of this liquefaction which is making my wheel skate about and forcing me to walk as soon as I come to an uphill slope. I come to them constantly and they are longer than the downhill ones. So I have all the time in the world to watch out for the little white hectometric cubes buried in the grass, but I count them backwards, from 9 down, so that I can really gnaw away at the distance and, at each yellow milestone, I put my head between my arms in the hollow of the handlebars, and their horns put the final touches to the impression of a winded old buffalo created by my rucksack. Thus I imitate the obtuse fatalism of cows and even derive some satisfaction from it. The cows don't move; they don't nibble; they just stand there with their feet apart in the middle of these meadows, among dense woodland where it's the rain that nibbles away with much din and where I have uttered dreadful blasphemies against the heavens, against my vehicle and the entire region. This is perhaps why the mountain refuses my chocolate. But what has been uttered cannot be taken back and I start off again, my hope no less obstinate than the rain. Another short downhill slope. The momentum I gain from it doesn't get me very far, but nearly as far as a shelter ingeniously put together out of an old car roof and sturdy trunks of rustic hazelnut wood. Inside is the original car seat, covered like the ground in a scattering of hay, packed down hard. I install myself here for a quarter of an hour, I strut about, casting a scornful eye on the flat summit the gods have refused me, listening to their monody of Celtic water crashing down on the metal awning. O gods, I think that we have come to the point where it is fair to halve shares: so I munch a few biscuits and more than half the bar of chocolate. But this act of betrayal quickly leads me to regrettable comparisons between this big and essentially overestimated hill and others that have never caused me so much bother, like Saint-Sernin or Mont Saint-Vincent. It is true that it was not raining, or raining less, and that I have my roots in that region. Whereas here, from the very start, I was patently up against spatial and climatic xenophobia. In the small town where I intend to turn off to complete my pilgrimage, people themselves will none the less be as courteous as usual. I mean that in the bistro into which I explode like a water-bomb, nobody shows surprise or curiosity nor do they affect indifference. I ask for a large rum and I get it at once, though unhurriedly; then I ask the way: it is pointed out to me at once, without a word or gesture too many. So off I set. Another eighteen kilometres on the national highway amid the in-breaths and spray of lorries, before I can once again see the Ménez Hom like a sphinx above the illuminated bay, painted on wet silk like Japan.

With a reticence due to the state of my German, I point out two cakes to the ladies in the shop and they are brought over later to the corner where I am sitting. I am next to the window and can see the shine on the roof of the cathedral. I rather dread the moment when the bells start ringing. But the sky is quiet for the moment, pale like a vault. There is a shout buried deep in this tranquil light. Snuggled into soft upholstery and the dark smell of chocolate, I start thinking about other Easter mornings in other cities when this stupor of the Resurrection already overcame me. They came to the tomb, so we are told by Matthew, Mark and Luke, and they found it empty. It all took place at daybreak, in a flurry of silence and solitude, secretly. Then the sun turned pale on the dust of His sandals. I still don't understand it. Should there have been more sense of drama and glorious thunder about it? No, no. I think that His eyes blinked in the meagre intensity of dawn and that He took His first steps with the dazed consciousness of a man released from prison, going off any old how along the rails staring at the hollow in his hands, feeling his beard grow. My train leaves in an hour or two. Time enough, before the bells start to bombard us, to make my way through the parks beneath the monumental, numb stupor of the Habsburgs. In a state of embarrassment caused by my knapsack, I leave without seeking a smile from the pastry shop ladies in their black and white uprightness.

In the almost empty brasserie people scent me out with a certain caution because I have selected a table near the window, set apart, and from it I can see the Adolphe Bridge spanning the tops of plunging trees, the redoubts on the other bank and the medieval pasteboard Savings Bank, flattened by floodlights. So that is where I was a while ago with my small suitcase, alone in the darkness. Seated on the ground, I smelled the leaves, that strong decoction of heat in the none the less freezing air. I have been stopping there regularly for years now, at whatever time of year, punctually awaiting someone else who is absent, with the result that the place half way up the hill always seems new to me, because of the recurrence of this expectant waiting, but I don't linger there for too long. In fact I don't linger anywhere; I am always immediately somewhere else in my imagination. There is the moment of arrival and the moment of departure. Between the two I quickly lose the sense of my existence; I am perhaps the someone else who awaits me, and this idea or a noise on the bridge takes me out of myself; recurring memories frighten me. At this moment I would like to add up the accounts of my life of expenditure and saving, of filth and pasteboard, but it comes to nothing. At times I have rebuilt everything in the throes of retroactive expectation, at others I have crushed everything beneath the obvious presence of despair. This evening there is a respite in my theatre: taking time as it comes. I am brought a plate of raw ham and some Reisling in a heavy glass. Outside, the moon runs along without falling down, like a little empty clog above the gorge. I have had to be careful more than once when I went across the gorge. Perhaps it will end in disaster, this panic-stricken lure of the Pétrusse, or perhaps not so disastrously: straight across, taking the quickest route, with almost no gap between departure and arrival, or what eludes me here – for it is already late and too late – the real meaning of my parable. For the time being I drink my Riesling, and I shall ask for another. Another glass and another moment. Thus from one tiny limit to the next, alone with the well-worn sky beneath a drum-shaped moon, in the comfortable empty space before things are set in motion and I start to believe that everything is beginning again.

And finally in an empty carriage, this couchette compartment where I install myself at Saint-Pierre-des-Corps. It is two in the morning but I cannot sleep. One last time, I have something like a brain seizure of speed and solitude, after days on the move. Then once I'm back in harness, I start to explode because the world is vast, the world is beautiful, from the hills of the Sarthe, turned to mist in the harmony of angels, to those thickets amid the excavations, full of debris and water more pungent than absinthe. I feel the heat once more and the sudden ice of evening in the valleys, at a time when nothing could have deflected me from my journey. And I can see the side of a small road in the Orne once again with that tank which appeared never to have been used and the three names of its crew forgotten on a brass nameplate. But I planted a salvo of poppies in the gun-barrel for them. Likewise forgotten is the name of the small town where I am buying another straw hat, Good day, Madame, what lovely weather we're having. It is midday and I am neither hungry nor thirsty, but filled with a love that grows as I nourish it. The streets of this forgotten hole, like those of Argos and Thebes, lie low beneath the fire of the god that shrivels the hearts of dogs and poultry in back yards (and my own heart now merges with the movement of metal, the sands and diamonds of the Loire sleeping naked beneath us).